Why the Undocumented Belong to America

Why the Undocumented Belong to America

The Experience of Rosa Robles Loreto and Eleven Million Others

DENISE HOLLEY

ISBN: 1541113217
ISBN 13: 9781541113213
Library of Congress Control Number: 2017902657
CreateSpace Independent Publishing Platform
North Charleston, South Carolina

Contents

Introduction

Republican candidate Donald Trump barreled through the November 2016 campaign and election and won the presidency on a pro–US worker, anti-immigrant platform. My heart sinks to realize how many of my fellow Americans believe Latino and Muslim immigrants threaten their well-being. My guess is that many of Trump's supporters live far from the border between the United States and Mexico and don't come into contact with immigrants in our cities. How else could they write off entire populations as less deserving of the blessings of liberty and opportunity we all share in America?

I begin with a narrative about Rosa Robles Loreto, whose fifteen-month stay in sanctuary at my church in Tucson, Arizona, focused national attention on the dilemma of hardworking, undocumented parents. While driving to work or school or going shopping, these people can get stopped for a minor traffic violation and end up in Border Patrol custody, even without a criminal record. Deporting an immigrant who has lived in the United States for a long time is a wrenching experience. It can leave children without a parent, a family without a breadwinner, and family members who are citizens and permanent residents heartbroken.

Detaining and deporting undocumented people violates the personal and religious beliefs of many Americans. A few churches have revived the sanctuary movement of the 1980s, when volunteers protected Central Americans who faced death if they returned to their countries. My church, Southside Presbyterian Church in Tucson, a pioneer sanctuary church, hosted two Mexican immigrants who faced deportation orders in 2014.

The estimated 11.3 million undocumented residents in the United States form part of this country. Their lives and their labor are woven into the fabric of our daily lives. They belong to America because they share our values. They embody the American dream of opportunity as surely as the immigrants who arrived from Europe in the late nineteenth and early twentieth centuries. These forebears of many US citizens arrived penniless on our shores with only their hopes and their willing hands. Why can't the immigrants of today follow the same path?

Unlike the European immigrants of yesterday, people from Mexico, Central America, and some Asian nations face a quota system that makes them wait years to enter the United States. For some, it's impossible. But economic forces line up to urge Mexicans and Central Americans northward—the push of poverty and violence and the pull of better-paying, relatively unskilled jobs in the United States. These economic migrants often risk their lives crossing the Southwestern desert to perform the dull, dirty, and dangerous jobs Americans don't want.

Undocumented immigrants bring their strong work ethic and fill jobs in the orchards, fields, slaughterhouses, and packing sheds that put food on American tables. Some work the bottom rungs of the hospitality industry, cleaning hotel rooms and washing dishes, while others carve out a living in landscaping and construction. Some have worked their way up to better jobs but face the requirement for documents their employers must copy and keep on file to avoid fines.

When the 1986 Immigration Reform and Control Act (IRCA) created an "amnesty" program, 2.7 million unauthorized residents came forward, paid a fee, learned basic English, and became legal residents. Many traveled the road to citizenship. Today, those who were legalized in 1987 and 1988 have integrated so well into our society that they are indistinguishable from other legal residents and US citizens.

Most unauthorized immigrants want to legalize their status and get right with the law, but there is currently no way to do this. It has been thirty years since IRCA opened a pathway. In 2013, the US House of Representatives passed an overhaul of our broken immigration system, but the bill stalled in the Senate. President Obama resorted to an executive order in 2012 to allow young undocumented people brought to the United States as children to file for temporary legal residency (the Deferred Action for Childhood Arrivals, or DACA, program).

Although immigrants from many countries enter illegally or overstay their visas, the political focus is always on Mexico. Now immigration from our next-door neighbor has slowed and even reversed. A labor shortage looms in the United States as millions of baby boomers retire. We should encourage immigrants who already live here to pursue education and training to fill skilled jobs and contribute more to our tax base and Social Security system. The time is ripe to halt most deportations and to open a path to legal status for the millions of people who want to belong to America.

1

Rosa Takes Sanctuary

It was never supposed to go on this long.

Rosa Robles Loreto packed an overnight bag and moved into a small room at Southside Presbyterian Church in Tucson on August 7, 2014, seeking sanctuary from a deportation order. She thought she would be able to return to her home and housecleaning jobs in a matter of days or weeks. Daniel Neyoy Ruiz, the previous sanctuary seeker at the church, got a stay of his deportation order in less than a month.

But in the fall of 2015, the undocumented Mexican mother, then forty-two, still lived in the little room at Southside with its bunk beds, refrigerator, microwave, and computer. Her life turned upside down. Instead of rising at 4:30 a.m. to start her busy day as a working mother, Rosa stayed up late into the night. When sleep wouldn't come, she read her Bible, listened to Christian music, and watched inspirational movies online, often until 4:00 a.m.

"They were my refuge," Rosa said, a way to take her mind off her boys, Gerardo Jr., eleven, and José Emiliano, eight, and everything she missed about them. She and her husband, Gerardo Grijalva, decided the boys should live at home to keep their lives as normal as possible. They showed up on weekends, often in uniforms and fresh from baseball games, and sat with her during the Sunday worship service.

One element at a time, Rosa's old life slipped away—the housecleaning jobs, her boys' baseball games, and her Catholic parish where she volunteered and where her sons were studying catechism and preparing for their first Holy Communion.

While she waited, Rosa drew spiritual strength from the Protestant church that took her in. Its unique style was unfamiliar at first but warm and welcoming. Every Sunday, she worshipped in the kiva (the sunken Hopi-style sanctuary), usually with her family. Sometimes she read a Bible verse in Spanish from the pulpit, a tradition in the multicultural church. With time on her hands, she sought ways to be useful. She chopped vegetables for the twice-weekly meal for the homeless and people in need. She listened to English-language tapes and conversed with the volunteers who accompanied her every evening and weekend. Once a month, she helped at an immigration clinic held at the church, encouraging other people trying to fend off deportation.

The high point of each day was the 7:00 p.m. prayer vigil. Sometimes visitors from local churches crowded into the fellowship hall, and other times just a few supporters came to pray with Rosa for her deliverance. Occasionally, a Catholic priest celebrated

Mass with her, and Bishop Gerald Kicanas of the Catholic Diocese of Tucson visited several times.

The wait for a resolution to her deportation case was "excruciating for [Rosa]," said Southside member Cecilia Valenzuela Gee, who helped coordinate a network of volunteers to stay with Rosa. "The vigils are a tremendous source of support for her."

Rosa lived in the calm eye of a hurricane over illegal immigration that swirled around Southside and the entire country. In the 1980s, Southside members sheltered undocumented Central Americans who risked death if they returned home. The church, under the leadership of the Reverend John Fife, became the cradle of the sanctuary movement. When a new sanctuary movement surfaced in the twenty-first century to protect immigrants from deportation, the Southside community decided—again—to offer protection.

"I think this [sanctuary] movement is grounded in faith and guided by the words of Jesus to keep families united," said Valenzuela Gee, who was raised Catholic. "This is the right thing to do."

Providing sanctuary has "deepened our sense of what hospitality is all about," said the Reverend Alison Harrington, pastor at Southside.

It also brought more people and publicity to the church and thrust Rosa into the national spotlight. Reporters and television crews interviewed Rosa and publicized her case locally and across the nation. As her time in sanctuary wore on, she became a local celebrity and a national symbol of the fractured, inconsistent US immigration policy.

Rosa never sought publicity, but she realizes she is a symbol. "It embarrasses me," she said about all the media attention, but "with my voice and my experience, I want to serve other families [who face deportation], because we are millions."

Rosa told me she hoped Americans wouldn't resent her and her family for wanting to settle in the United States sixteen years ago. "We immigrants don't come to take away anyone's rights," she said. "We simply come in search of opportunities." Someday, she would like to own a housecleaning business.

She spoke warmly of her circle of Southside supporters and especially Keep Tucson Together, a working group of the humanitarian aid organization No More Deaths. KTT took her immigration case to the courts and then to the streets. "I fell into blessed hands," she said about the group whose attorney, Margo Cowan, pursued her case for several years and never gave up.

In September 2014, Rosa's supporters persuaded first the Pima County Board of Supervisors and then the Tucson City Council to pass resolutions of support for Rosa as a valued member of the community. In January 2015, the *Arizona Daily Star* in Tucson called on the Department of Homeland Security (DHS) to close Rosa's deportation case. Church members and supporters flooded DHS, President Obama's office, and Immigration and Customs Enforcement (ICE) with hundreds of letters and e-mail messages.

Cowan repeatedly appealed to ICE for a reprieve. The response was silence.

"When we started in August [with Rosa], I never dreamed we'd still be here at Christmas," Cowan told the Southside congregation on December 14, 2014.

2

What Does It Take to Melt the Heart of ICE?

R osa's legal troubles began in September 2010 when she hit an orange cone in a construction zone while driving to a house-cleaning job. She always drove carefully and kept her eyes on the road so she would never attract the attention of a police officer. But suddenly, here was a sheriff's vehicle in her rearview mirror, flashing its lights for her to pull over.

With her heart pounding, Rosa handed her Mexican driver's license to the deputy. He asked Rosa if she was in the country illegally, and she told him the truth. She pleaded with him to just issue her a ticket. He called the Border Patrol.

When Rosa refused to sign a voluntary departure form to be deported, she was taken to a detention center in Eloy, Arizona. She endured sixty days in prison without visitors until her family bonded her out for $3,000.

"I didn't sign anything because I wanted to see a judge first," Rosa said.

Rosa hired a lawyer and fought her deportation in court. But her lawyer never asked the court to close her case, an option under the policy of prosecutorial discretion. In September 2012, she returned to court and got bad news: she had to leave the country by November 27. She turned to Keep Tucson Together (KTT), a local organization that helps immigrants close their deportation cases, and Margo Cowan, its attorney.

For a year and a half, Cowan tried to get Rosa's case reviewed. But in the summer of 2014, Rosa received a letter from Immigration and Customs Enforcement (ICE) that ordered her to leave the country by August 8. She came to Southside with her overnight bag on August 7.

Southside had already given sanctuary from deportation to Daniel Neyoy Ruiz and his wife and son in the spring of 2014. In just under a month, ICE issued him a stay of deportation and the family went home. When the stay expired in June 2015, Daniel briefly entered sanctuary at another church. Then ICE granted him another one-year reprieve.

Why did he get a stay and Rosa did not? "Daniel has a US-citizen child and Rosa doesn't," Cowan said.

Rosa and Gerardo grew up in Hermosillo, Sonora, and sometimes visited a relative in Tucson on tourist visas. When they discovered they could earn far more doing domestic and gardening work in the United States than at her bank job and his job in a construction office in Mexico, they returned to Tucson in 1999 and overstayed their visas.

But the couple returned to Hermosillo for the births of their children. "We only came here to work and not to ask for help from the government," Rosa said. It made sense to her to give birth in her hometown where her family lived and where the hospital expenses were lower. So their sons were also Mexican citizens with no legal claim to stay in the United States without a visa.

When President Obama announced his new executive action on immigration on November 20, 2014, Rosa and Gerardo fixed their eyes on a television in the kiva at Southside, waiting breathlessly to learn if the orders would include them. They did not. Only parents of US-born children or lawful permanent residents would benefit from Deferred Action for Parents of Americans (DAPA).

But Obama expanded the age range of those included in Deferred Action for Childhood Arrivals (DACA), so younger children, like Rosa's two sons, could qualify. Just before they mailed their application packets, a federal court issued a temporary injunction on February 16, 2015, halting DAPA and the DACA expansion but not the original DACA program. In June 2016, a divided US Supreme Court sent the case back to the appellate court, which meant the programs could not go forward.

In February 2015, with Rosa still in sanctuary, KTT launched a grassroots campaign to blanket Tucson neighborhoods with signs bearing a drawing of Rosa and her family with the words We Stand with Rosa. Valenzuela Gee and other Southside members spoke on behalf of Rosa at local Catholic and Protestant churches, she said.

They delivered hundreds of Rosa signs for parishioners to post in their yards. By the fall of 2015, volunteers had distributed some 9,600 signs to decorate homes and businesses around Tucson.

Three immigrants who sought church sanctuary in 2014 came to Southside in February 2015 to encourage Rosa and to speak at a community event. Neyoy Ruiz joined Francisco Pérez Cordova, who took sanctuary at Saint Francis in the Hills United Methodist Church in Tucson from September to December 2014. Angela Navarro traveled from Philadelphia where she had lived in sanctuary from November 2014 to January 2015. All three had emerged with their deportation orders lifted or cases closed.

All Rosa could get from ICE was a letter that said she was not a priority for deportation. But her case was still open, and the deportation order still hung over her head.

"Not having a paper doesn't mean I'm not of the US," Rosa said after she had spent a year in sanctuary. "I don't believe God rejects anyone for being American or Mexican."

Rosa said she told her boys that if you have faith, then everything is possible. "I still have faith and hope that God will grant me liberty."

Nearly one hundred of her supporters gathered outside the downtown library in the midday heat on August 7, 2015, to mark Rosa's one-year anniversary in sanctuary. The guest of honor could not see the long half circle of signs with her name or hear the words of encouragement from elected officials and the applause.

For her safety, she had to remain behind the gates of the church courtyard.

After 461 days in sanctuary, the long-awaited word from the Department of Homeland Security (DHS) arrived in early November 2015. Pastor Harrington waited until the Sunday worship service on November 8, when the children gathered in front of the pulpit. She recounted Rosa's reasons for coming to live at the church and then declared, "This week, Rosa is going home!"

Whoops and cheers filled the kiva, and people jumped to their feet in a standing ovation for Rosa and her family. The boys, hearing the news for the first time, hugged their mother and danced around her. The family and Southside members wiped tears of joy from their eyes.

Three days later, photographers clustered in the center of the kiva as Rosa's family entered for a press conference. The crowd of Southsiders and supporters rose to their feet, chanting "Rosa!" and turned the event into a celebration.

Cowan announced a confidential agreement with DHS to allow Rosa to live without fear of deportation. "I can't talk about it," Cowan told the audience. "But...she's fine, she's protected."

A few weeks earlier, Cowan had represented Rosa's husband, Gerardo Grijalva, in court and successfully closed his deportation case. Now he no longer had to look over his shoulder when he drove to his landscaping job or took his boys to baseball practice where he coached a team.

"Rosa, this lady, is every mom," Cowan said. "This guy [Gerardo] is every dad. They're us. When we have our [legal] clinics here at Southside, we call it Keep Tucson Together."

Finally, Rosa took the microphone. "First of all, I want to thank God for this great struggle and experience because without the faith I have in him and the strength from your prayers, we would not have arrived at this day," she said. She poured out her gratitude to Cowan, KTT, all her supporters, and especially to Harrington.

"Besides being a pastor, she is a mother, and as a mother, I know what this struggle meant to her," Rosa said. "The struggle continues," she added and vowed to keep working for other undocumented immigrants.

Harrington asked those who had posted Rosa signs to decorate them with balloons and flowers. "Don't take them down," she said. "There are so many Rosas in our community."

Cowan emphasized that "today is only a beginning...We don't stop until nobody in America has to live in fear."

As the family walked out into the sunshine, trailed by José Emiliano's teammates in their baseball uniforms, the people in the sanctuary serenaded them with the hymn "We Will Go Out with Joy."

3

Why Is It So Difficult to Immigrate Legally?

If Rosa and her husband had traveled from Europe to America by ship in the late nineteenth or early twentieth centuries, then they would probably have been welcomed at the dock, processed, and given papers to work. Today, many aspiring immigrants who seek safety and a chance to build a new life in the United States find the door bolted.

In an ideal world, all the people who want to immigrate to the United States just get into a line and wait their turn, and eventually, every qualifying foreigner gets a green card. Apparently, many Americans hold this belief. They regard those who cross the US-Mexico border illegally as line jumpers who deserve to be deported because they don't play by the rules.

But there is no actual line to get into, according to the Migration Policy Institute (MPI).

"Contrary to popular belief, there is not a single 'line' that leads to lawful permanent residence," wrote Claire Bergeron of MPI, but rather there are multiple pathways. "Wait times can vary dramatically—as much as two decades—depending on the applicant's visa category and country of nationality."[1]

Every year, would-be immigrants file a snowstorm of applications with the US Citizenship and Immigration Services (USCIS), but only a fraction can squeeze into the few avenues open.

For starters, you must have a US citizen or legal permanent resident (LPR) or an employer to sponsor you. If you are the minor child, spouse, or parent of a citizen, then you're in luck. There is no limit on the number of visas in that category, and you should be able to join your citizen family member in the United States. But other family members—adult children, siblings, or any family member of an LPR—endure years of waiting for an immigrant visa in the family preference system.

"Every year, we immigrate about a million people," said Sharon Rummery, public affairs officer for USCIS in San Francisco. But, Rummery explained, to become one of those lucky one million, a would-be immigrant must usually fit into one of these five categories:

1. Have relatives living in the United States with good immigration standing (citizen or legal permanent resident). About two-thirds of immigrants enter under this category.

---

1 Claire Bergeron, "Going to the Back of the Line: A Primer on Lines, Visa Categories, and Wait Times," Migration Policy Institute, March 2013, http://www.migrationpolicy.org/research/going-back-line-primer-lines-visa-categories-and-wait-times.

2. Have an employer petition for your entry. This category is usually for skilled workers in demand by US companies and does not include seasonal workers.

3. Have a refugee visa. Refugee visas are issued before arrival in the United States to persons who are outside their country and are unable or unwilling to return home because they fear serious harm. A refugee must apply for adjustment of status after living in the United States for one year.

4. Be granted asylum. Asylum is granted for persons here in the United States, or present at the border, who left their country because of a well-founded fear of persecution based on race, religion, nationality, political opinion, or special social group. If the status is granted, then the asylee can apply for adjustment of status after one year. (That means they'll be lawful, permanent residents and can one day become US citizens.)

5. Obtain a diversity visa, also called the green card lottery. Once a year, the State Department makes up to fifty thousand immigrant visas available, drawn from random selection among all entries to people from countries not already well represented in the United States. (This would exclude anyone from Mexico and many other countries.)

An immigration judge can grant immigrant status to a person who is in deportation proceedings, Rummery said. To be eligible, you must have lived in the United States for ten years, be a person of good moral character, and have an immediate relative who would suffer severe hardship if you were removed.

"When you petition for an eligible relative who's not an immediate family member, the clock starts to run," Rummery said.

The State Department sets an annual minimum family-sponsored preference limit of 226,000 visas and at least fourteen thousand employment-based visas each year, and no one country can take more than 7 percent of the visas. So the clock may have to run for a long time.

"Countries such as Mexico that have very sizeable immigrant and later-generation populations in the US thus have far more de-mand for visas than the 7 percent per-country cap permits," wrote Michelle Mittelstadt, director of communications and public af-fairs for MPI, in an e-mail. "For example, 7 percent of the sixty-five thousand visas allowed annually for siblings of US citizens who are twenty-one and older means just 4,550 visas...Backlogs would quickly build up, as they do for Mexico, India, and China in particular."

Mexicans and Filipinos face long waits for many family visas, going back to applications they filed in the 1990s, according to a chart in the Visa Bulletin issued by the US Department of State in July 2016.

In 2013, more than four million people, eligible for visas but waiting for their priority date to become current, were jamming the system according to Bergeron at MPI. She calculated it would take nineteen years to clear the existing backlogs in the family-based preference categories. But that assumes something unlikely: that no new petitions get filed during this time.

An unknown number of people waiting for these visas live il-legally in the United States, according to Bergeron. When their long-awaited priority date comes up, they must leave the United

States and return to their home countries to pick up the visa. But that trip will trigger a provision of the Illegal Immigration Reform and Immigrant Responsibility Act of 1996 that bars would-be immigrants from coming back to the United States for ten years if they lived unlawfully in the United States for more than a year. (Those who resided between 180 days and one year receive a three-year bar.)

So after years of living in limbo, if an undocumented person eligible for a green card tries to legalize his or her status and takes the final step at a US consulate in the country of origin, then he or she is effectively deported (see chapter 6 on the 1996 immigration law.) But, according to Mittelstadt, if the person can demonstrate "extreme hardship" to a US citizen or LPR child or spouse, then he or she may be able to get a waiver.

Until recently, one fortunate group didn't have to jump through all these hoops in the US immigration system to gain legal status: Cubans. The United States rolled out the welcome mat for Cuban nationals who fled the Communist island and reached American soil. (It was called the "wet foot, dry foot" policy.) Under the Cuban Adjustment Act of 1996, Cuban natives or citizens and their spouses and children could get a green card after one year of residence in the United States. There was no need to qualify under the requirements of Section 245 of the Immigration and Nationality Act, according to the USCIS, so a Cuban did not need a sponsoring family member or an employer to apply for permanent residency.

Former President Obama rescinded this policy on January 12, 2017, as part of normalizing relations with Cuba. Now Cubans who arrive without a visa and do not qualify for asylum will be subject to removal just like migrants from any other country.

This former privileged status may explain the political divide between Cubans and Latinos from Mexico and Central America and their US-born family members. Ted Cruz and Marco Rubio, 2016 Republican presidential candidates, are Cuban Americans whose families came to the United States legally. During the campaign, they both took a hard line on any reforms that would help undocumented residents from other countries adjust their immigration status.

4

How Migration Became a Crime

The boy who would grow up to become sheriff of Santa Cruz County, Arizona, was born "across the line" in Nogales, Sonora, in 1943. Tony Estrada remembers a fluid border between the United States and Mexico when people would crawl through gaps in the fence. On fiesta days, immigration agents would open the ports of entry so families could cross and celebrate together.

His father, Jesús Estrada, crossed into Nogales, Arizona, and put his carpentry skills to work. "He was a jack of all trades," Estrada said. When his father worked for the Ahumada Brothers, nailing boxes together to ship machinery, he got a letter of support from his employer, and the family with four sons immigrated to the United States when Estrada was a toddler. A fifth son was born in Arizona, a US citizen. The other family members easily got their green (permanent resident) cards, and Estrada became a naturalized US citizen at twenty-one.

Under current immigration policy, it's doubtful the Estrada family could have immigrated legally.

"At that time, nobody was focusing on illegal immigration," Estrada said. He heard the term *mojados* (wetbacks), but it wasn't a crime to cross the border from Mexico into the United States.

"Up until the revision of immigration law in 1965, there was a free flow of migrants across the Mexican border," said Alan Kraut, professor of history at American University in Washington, DC. "After the 1965 act, there were hemispheric quotas, plus there was a limit on how many people each country could send. That's where the criminalization came in."

On its face, the Immigration and Nationality Act of 1965 was a bold step forward. It swept away the national quota system that had been in effect since 1924, which favored immigrants from Western Europe. It lifted bans on Asians and Africans and quotas on Eastern and Southern Europeans and parceled out visas equally to each country.

The law tried to end prejudice in the US immigration system, wrote Douglas S. Massey in the *Washington Post*. But it left our next-door neighbor, Mexico, with a severe shortage of visas for the thousands of Mexican workers who migrated seasonally to jobs in the United States.[2]

---

2 Douglas S. Massey, "How a 1965 Immigration Reform Created Illegal Immigration," *Washington Post*, September 25, 2015, http://www.washingtonpost. com/posteverything/wp/2015/09/25/how-a-1965-immigration-reform-created-illegal-immigration/?utm term=.cc5674aeb647. Massey is the Henry G. Bryant professor of sociology and public affairs at Princeton University and codirector of the Mexican Migration Project.

Around the same time, in 1964, the United States ended its *bracero* (guest worker) program, which had allowed Mexicans to work legally in US agriculture and then return home.

"The result was a progressive militarization of our southern border," Massey wrote. "Although little had changed in practical terms in the years after 1965—the same migrants were leaving the same communities to go to the same employers in the same US states in about the same numbers—now the migrants were 'illegal' and hence by definition 'lawbreakers' and 'criminals.'"[3]

In Nogales, Estrada watched the changing picture of migration from Mexico as he carved out an early career with the Nogales Police Department. In 1992, he ran for Santa Cruz County sheriff and won, serving his first of seven terms. Estrada said that when he took office in 1993 "there were no *coyotes* [guides]" for people attempting to cross the border and only about seventy Border Patrol agents traversing Santa Cruz County.

All that changed in the mid-1990s, Estrada said. In 1994, the North American Free Trade Agreement (NAFTA) began to work its changes in the United States, Canada, and Mexico. Its proponents thought it would increase prosperity in all three countries by knocking down barriers to trade. It allowed products and capital to flow across the border—but not labor. Its effect in Mexico actually spurred migration across the US border, according to National Public Radio reporter Ted Robbins.[4]

---

3 Ibid.

4 Ted Robbins, "Wave of Illegal Immigrants Gains Speed after NAFTA," National Public Radio, December 26, 2013, http://www.npr.org/2013/12/26/257255787/wave-of-illegal-immigrants-gains-speed-after-nafta. This piece was presented on the eve of NAFTA's twentieth anniversary.

Robbins explained that under NAFTA, the Mexican government dropped the corn subsidy that sustained small farmers. Tariffs were phased out, and cheaper corn from the US heartland flooded Mexico. Unable to compete and stay in agriculture, an estimated two million Mexican farmworkers left the countryside for big cities.

Many unemployed Mexicans migrated north to seek work in the *maquiladoras* (factories owned by foreigners, usually US companies) along the border, Estrada said. When there weren't enough jobs, some of them surged north into the Arizona desert, hoping to find work on the US side. Estrada saw the population of Nogales, Sonora, swell from about forty thousand in the late 1970s to close to three hundred thousand today.

To deter the border crossers, the Immigration and Naturalization Services (INS, the precursor of ICE, Customs and Border Protection and USCIS under the Department of Homeland Security) built an opaque fence of military helicopter landing mats in 1994. It traveled the length of Nogales, Arizona, and didn't stop until it stretched into the remote desert.

"It seemed to be the purpose of the Border Patrol, to move them [migrants] out," Estrada said.

Researchers with the organizations No More Deaths and the *Coalición de Derechos Humanos* (Human Rights Coalition) in Tucson would agree. In a report released in December 2016, they wrote that since the mid-1990s, the Border Patrol's policy of prevention through deterrence has pushed migration into more remote corridors. This has caused many border-crossers to disappear in the desert.[5]

Reports began to filter into Estrada's office about assault, rape, and murder in the borderlands, as coyotes and bandits preyed on vulnerable travelers. "We take a report and investigate," he said. But usually hours and days had elapsed since the alleged crime occurred, and often, the victim could not pinpoint the location.

Some migrants survive the crimes, elude the Border Patrol, and continue their journey north because "their expectations are so great," the sheriff said. Many have little to return to at home in the interior of Mexico or in Central American countries plagued with poverty, persecution, corruption, and gang violence.

Others succumb to the bone-dry desert. "One year [about ten years ago], we found two dozen bodies or skeletal remains," Estrada said.

People desperate to work or reunite with family in the United States are not deterred from crossing, according to the No More Deaths and *Derechos Humanos* researchers. Many are found dead, especially in southern Arizona. In June 2016, an unprecedented twenty-five sets of human remains were found in southern Arizona and sent to the Pima County Forensic Science Center. In July 2016, another twenty-four bodies were recovered. For fiscal year 2016, ending September 30, 2016, the total reached 145 bodies found in those areas. These people could have died crossing during this

---

5 "Disappeared: How US Border Enforcement Agencies Are Fueling a Missing Persons Crisis," No More Deaths, December 2016, http://www.thedisappearedreport.org.

year or years earlier before their remains were finally located in 2015 or 2016.[6]

As it became riskier to cross the border, more Mexican workers stayed in the United States year-round, and their spouses and children migrated north to join them, noted Douglas Massey. "In short, shifts in US immigration policies transformed a circular flow of male workers from Mexico going to a few states into a settled population of families living in 50 states, including 11 million undocumented people."[7]

In a different report, Massey and two coauthors point out how stepped-up enforcement made Mexican migrants think twice about returning home and then risking another crossing.

"Border enforcement, of course, does nothing to address the economic drivers of migration—persistent labor demand and high wages in the United States and an abundant labor supply and low wages in Mexico—nor does it take into account the existence of well-developed networks able to support and sustain undocumented border crossing and thus circumvent enforcement efforts," Massey and his coauthors wrote.[8]

"It [enforcement] created an industry for the cartels," Estrada said. During the 1990s, drug shipments to the United States escalated. Increased scrutiny at the ports of entry between the two

---

6 Figures obtained by Ed McCullough, member of the Tucson (Arizona) Samaritans, from the Pima County Forensic Science Center.

7 Massey, "How a 1965 Immigration Reform Created Illegal Immigration."

8 Douglas S. Massey, Karen A. Pren, and Jorge Durand, "Why Border EnforcementBackfired," *American Journal of Sociology*, 121, no. 5 (2016): 1557–1600, doi:10.1086, http://www.journals.uchicago.edu/doi/abs/10.1086/684200.

countries drove the drug transport business underground—literally. In 1995, law officers in Nogales discovered the first of what would become at least 110 tunnels that Mexican cartels had bored between the two cities named Nogales.

"We have nobody to blame but ourselves," Estrada said. "They [the cartels] saw a great market in the US." Eventually, they developed a side business of trafficking migrants through the borderlands.

With only 5 percent of the world's population, the United States consumes about 50 percent of its illegal drugs, Estrada said. "Illegal immigration pales compared with the drug problem we have as a nation." He stressed, "People should come here legally." But many immigrants from Mexico "are coming from extreme poverty, and [without paperwork] they have no chance of getting a visa." Estrada urged federal officials to go after criminal aliens, not families striving for a better life.

"I believe this nation is big enough and rich enough and powerful enough to take these eleven million [undocumented residents] out of the shadows," Estrada said. The immigrants display courage and a strong work ethic, and they are willing to make sacrifices for their families, qualities that can contribute to this country.

Estrada never forgot his humble beginnings in Mexico. "I wasn't born here. I was allowed here, and I made the best of it," he said. "I never imagined I would become one of three Hispanic sheriffs in Arizona. It was a dream come true."

5

A Chance of a Lifetime— the 1986 Amnesty Law

In 1987, thousands of people stopped hiding their illegal residency in the United States. They lined up at offices of community organizations to grasp a rare opportunity to gain legal status in their adopted country.

The 1986 Immigration Reform and Control Act (IRCA) coupled a carrot—amnesty for longtime illegal residents and farmworkers—with a stick—employer sanctions for bosses who continued to hire those who didn't qualify. For the first time, employers had to verify permission to work for all employees or face fines.

Its theory was simple: if we secure the US-Mexico border and curb the magnet of quick employment for migrants in the country illegally by penalizing their employers, then we can allow undocumented people who meet certain requirements to apply for legal residency. The bill was widely known as the amnesty law.

Backers hoped IRCA would halt the stream of illegal migrants, primarily from Mexico, flowing across the US border. It didn't, perhaps because enforcement of employer sanctions was gradual and sporadic. Many people regard IRCA as a failure. Now the term *amnesty* gets a bad rap whenever Congress debates any measure to reform the immigration system.

But I believe IRCA was a resounding success for 2.7 million immigrants. Those who qualified and presented themselves to immigration officials gained a chance for better education and jobs and an end to fear of deportation. Today, these people have integrated into the fabric of American life, just as European immigrants did in the late nineteenth and early twentieth centuries.

The original bill allowed people who had lived in the United States continuously since January 1, 1982, to apply for legal status. Applicants had to prove their residency, pass a background check, and show they had the financial resources to avoid becoming a public charge. They also had to pony up fees of $185 per adult and $50 per child.

But growers worried that their migrant workers, who often traveled back to Mexico for the winter, would not qualify. Some of them persuaded Congress to let farmworkers who had worked for at least ninety days in perishable US crops during the last season (May 1985 to May 1986) gain legal status under the Special Agricultural Worker (SAW) program.

IRCA required the undocumented to overcome their fears and to learn to trust the Immigration and Naturalization Service

(INS) to handle their applications. At the same time, the bill gave employers a reason to mistrust the INS, since its agents could show up at any time and check hiring records.

A grape grower I met when I lived in Sonoma County, California, put it this way: "Now the INS won't come looking for illegals," she said. "They'll come looking for employers."

Congress passed the law late in 1986. The legalization program didn't get up and running until May 1987. At the time, I was working for California Human Development Corporation (CHDC) in Santa Rosa, California, a nonprofit that used funds from the US Department of Labor to train farmworkers for more stable jobs. Since undocumented workers were shut out of these programs, CHDC jumped on board when the INS contracted with community organizations to screen amnesty applicants.

I showed up with my camera and notebook the first day CHDC took in applicants. A group of men sat on the porch of our rural office, fingering their paperwork and talking quietly. Then an INS van drove up to the building. A sudden look of fear crossed the men's faces. Some of them appeared ready to bolt. But once the agents began talking with CHDC staff, the men slowly unwound and waited their turns to apply for a shot at legal residency.

They were among the first of 1.3 million farmworkers who applied for legal status in the United States between 1987 and 1988, according to figures from the Migration Policy Institute (MPI). Another 1.75 million immigrants who had lived more than five years in the United States also tendered their applications. About

2.7 million people eventually qualified and gained legal status through IRCA.

In 2006, I interviewed several amnesty beneficiaries in Napa County, California. They included a man who bought a home in a neighborhood with other working-class Latinos and became president of their homeowners' association. Another was a woman enrolled in community college who hoped to transfer to a university and become a teacher.

Ben Monterroso crossed the US border to Los Angeles without documents in 1977. He was a wide-eyed teenager eager to work hard and save his money. In five years, he figured, he could return to Guatemala with a car, a truck, a motorcycle, and $20,000 to start a business. "We came to this country to build our American dream," he said.

It didn't work out that way. Forty years later, he is not only a US citizen but also heads an organization with offices in Arizona, California, Colorado, Florida, Nevada, and Texas that motivates Latinos to vote and to participate in politics. In September 2015, as executive director of *Mi Familia Vota* (My Family Votes), he was invited to the White House to meet Pope Francis.

The 1986 immigration law played a pivotal role in Monterroso's journey to success. As a new immigrant, he found a job in a furniture factory that paid him $2.00 per hour, below the minimum wage of $2.25, and no time and a half for overtime. When the factory burned down, he delivered pizzas and worked as a carpenter. In 1979, he landed a job as a janitor that paid $6.02 per hour (when the minimum wage was $3.35) and provided health insurance and paid sick time, holidays, and vacation.

"Before then, I never made more than minimum wage," Monterroso said. He quickly learned that a few dollars deducted from his pay supported the union that negotiated those work benefits. "I became aware that workers have rights in this country."

In 1981, he married a woman from El Salvador and went to work as a union organizer for the Service Employees International Union (SEIU). Monterroso said, "When my first daughter was born, I put my original dream on the shelf."

When IRCA passed, it was an answer to his prayers, "knowing people who suffered more than me, not having documents," Monterroso said. Most undocumented residents felt safer if they stayed under the radar of any government officials. "It took a lot of guts [for the first legalization applicants] to apply," he said. "I was afraid that instead of a line for coming out of the shadows, it could be a line to be deported."

When immigration officials handed Monterroso his temporary resident card, a sense of relief and freedom washed over him. No longer did he get startled when he saw a brown UPS van, thinking it was the INS looking for people to deport. "I felt finally that I was a real human being," Monterroso said.

He helped his wife and his brothers and sisters apply for the legalization program, and one brother later petitioned for their mother to immigrate to the United States. After five years as a legal permanent resident, Monterroso became a US citizen. "This country had given me so much," he said.

So why didn't IRCA stop illegal immigration? In August 2005, MPI outlined several reasons in a policy brief:

- Enforcement at the US-Mexico border was inadequate.
- The application requirements for legalization led to mixed-status families. Members who immigrated after the cutoff date in 1982 could not qualify for amnesty.
- There was no plan for those undocumented residents who did not qualify. "Those who did not legalize became the nucleus of the unauthorized population today," wrote the authors.
- IRCA generated an increase in applications to bring family members to the United States and overwhelmed the INS.
- Employment continued to drive unauthorized immigration, despite IRCA's employer sanctions. At the time the brief was written, more than 90 percent of unauthorized males in the US were employed.[9]

Michelle Mittelstadt, a spokeswoman for MPI, explained further in an e-mail message on March 11, 2016: "IRCA's legalization provisions took effect almost immediately, but the enforcement provisions with regards to employer sanctions and the hiring of unauthorized workers took years to roll out. Nearly three million people were legalized as a result of IRCA and gained green cards, but the law provided no pathway for these legalizing immigrants

---

9 Betsy Cooper and Kevin O'Neil, "Lessons from the Immigration Reform and Control Act of 1986," Migration Policy Institute, August 2005, http://www.migrationpolicy.org/research/lessons-immigration-reform-and-control-act-1986.

to bring relatives—spurring new illegal immigration as families sought to reunify."

Once the SAWs (agricultural workers) became legal permanent residents, "they were able to sponsor their families for immigration," Mittelstadt wrote on April 7, 2016. "But the reality is there were very few visas available for Mexicans. It wasn't until the 1990 Immigration Act that Congress set aside visas to deal with the backlog."

IRCA had a fiscal downside, according to researchers at the Center for Immigration Studies who tracked the costs to federal, state, and local governments over the first ten years of the program. The report stated that the newly legalized population received $102.1 billion in benefits but paid the government only $78 billion in taxes, due to their low educational levels and low wages. Moreover, legalized immigrants displaced some US-citizen workers from low-wage jobs, which caused them to rely on government assistance. In the wake of IRCA, Congress appropriated $3.5 billion to aid states with expenses related to the new legal residents through 1994, but that translated to only $1,167 per person. The author estimated the total cost to the government, including schooling for the residents' children, was $29,148 for each person legalized.[10]

This sounds costly, but consider these two facts:

American taxpayers contribute an average of $12,296 per year to educate a public-school student, according to the National

---

10 David Simcox, "Measuring the Fallout," Center for Immigration Studies, May 1997, http://cis.org/IRCAAmnesty-10YearReview.

Center for Education Statistics website. Do we balk at spending this much to prepare a US citizen for the workforce?

Most of the amnesty beneficiaries have children educated in the United States. Equipped with fluent English, these students graduated into service employment, skilled trades, business, and professional jobs. Surely, they contribute a higher share of taxes than their parents did to finance our public services and to support retired Americans. Citizens or not, these students represent an investment in our future.

6

How the 1996 Immigration
Law Divides Families

If the 1986 immigration law was a warm embrace for many un-documented residents, the Illegal Immigration Reform and Immigrant Responsibility Act of 1996 (IIRIRA) was a cold slap in the face. Ironically, a Republican president, Ronald Reagan, signed the 1986 bill into law, but the punitive 1996 law, which contained several reforms, passed under a Democratic president, Bill Clinton.

One of the provisions of the 1996 law turned a time-honored tradition on its head: no longer would marriage to a US citizen automatically offer a ticket to legal residency in the United States for any undocumented immigrant. In Section 301, the law erected a three-year bar to legal residency for any foreign national who had resided unlawfully in the United States for more than 180 days but less than one year. But if the immigrant had stayed unlawfully for more than one year (which is the case for the majority of undocumented people), then the penalty was a ten-year bar to reentry.

The law granted only a few exceptions for minors, asylum-seekers, and victims of domestic abuse.

Many couples learned the hard way.

In the mountain village of Leavenworth, Washington, mechanic Cody Havens fell in love with a Mexican woman who served him lunch every day at the Burger King drive-through window. In 2001, he asked her to marry him.

Teresa De Jesús Jiménez was intent on working when she traveled from Oaxaca, Mexico, in 1997, crossed the border without papers, and found two jobs in the Bavarian-themed tourist town. She owed medical bills from her late husband's illness and needed school supplies for her three children so they could continue past sixth grade. She never imagined she would find love again.

After their wedding, Cody petitioned the Immigration and Naturalization Service (INS) for legal status for his wife. In 2003, the couple traveled to the American consulate in Ciudad Juárez, Mexico, for Teresa's final interview. They carried letters of praise from Teresa's employers in Leavenworth. As they sat in the office, nervous but hopeful, a consular official delivered the worst possible news: Teresa was not eligible for legal residency because she had lived in the United States for more than a year, left to visit her children, and then reentered the country illegally. He confiscated her Washington driver's license and told her she was barred from the United States for ten years.

Teresa went back to her parents' home in Oaxaca, and Cody returned to Washington, heartbroken. He sought help from his congressman and a lawyer, without success. In 2004, he showed up at the *Wenatchee World*, where I worked as the family and faith reporter. He gave me Teresa's phone number in Oaxaca, and I interviewed her as well.

"What is happening to Cody and me is an injustice," Teresa told me. She desperately wanted to return to Washington with her children "so we can be a family."

Cody told me he visited his wife in Oaxaca and realized he could never support the family if he worked there as a mechanic. So he returned to his home and auto-repair shop in Washington.

"The only reason I get up in the morning is to get my wife back," he said.

In August 2004, we published a story about the couple's dilemma, with their wedding photo and a sidebar about how the ten-year bar from the United States affected other couples.[11]

"People think that marriage to a US citizen will enable them to immigrate," said Sharon Rummery, public affairs officer for US Citizenship and Immigration Services (USCIS) in San Francisco. But, she continued, if you entered the country without inspection, then you must return to your own country to pick up an immigrant visa. If eligible, then you can apply to adjust your status.

---

11 Denise Holley, "A Family Divided," *The Wenatchee World*, August 27, 2004, C1–2.

Cody Havens called USCIS to petition for legal status for Teresa and followed their instructions. The staff, perhaps unaware that Teresa had left the United States and returned, assured him it was a simple process and he didn't need an attorney.

"You don't want to leave the country without getting some advice from an immigration attorney," emphasized Andy Silverman, professor emeritus at the University of Arizona, where he taught immigration law for more than forty years.

The 1996 law allowed the attorney general to grant a waiver if the immigrant was the child or spouse of a citizen or permanent resident who would suffer extreme hardship if the family member were not admitted. Apparently, this waiver was not always granted.

The *Arizona Daily Star* in Tucson reported on the dilemma of Gloria de la Rosa of that city, who was stranded in Mexico in 2009 after she petitioned the USCIS for permanent legal status. She also traveled to Ciudad Juárez for her final interview. Consular officials barred her from returning to the United States for ten years because, years earlier, she had crossed the border illegally after her visa expired.[12]

Star reporter Perla Trevizo and Arizona Public Media reporter Fernanda Echavarri portrayed the disrupted lives of de la Rosa's four children, all US citizens like their father. The oldest, Jim, was a senior in high school, and the youngest, Bobby, was almost four

---

12 Perla Trevizo and Fernanda Echavarri, "Divided by Law," a front-page series of four articles in the *Arizona Daily Star* and feature stories on Arizona Public Media television, October 2015.

when their mother went to Mexico. His sister, Naomi, comforted him in her absence and when their ailing father was in the hospital.

Jim enlisted in the US Marine Corps and thrived in his mission. The second son, Bill, excelled in school and earned a scholarship to a university in Maine. Naomi worked hard to balance housework and homework, with her eye on going to college after she graduated. At the invitation of Congressman Raúl Grijalva, Bobby talked about his family's separation at an immigration forum at Pima Community College and later at a rally for Democratic presidential candidate Bernie Sanders in the summer of 2015.

On weekends, the family drives to Nogales, Sonora, to visit Gloria, who lives in a small apartment and cleans houses for a living. She often sends dishes of food home with her loved ones, but she can't come back and care for her eighty-two-year-old husband, not for four more years. So Jim reluctantly put his career as a marine on hold and returned home to look after his father so Bill could study across the country.

7

Deportation Wreaks Havoc with Lives of Immigrants

*Deportations destroy communities and disgrace
our faith values of justice, dignity, and hospitality.
They create a horrific scar across our country and
those in power must be held accountable for the
enormous destruction deportations have caused.*

—Statement from the New Sanctuary
Movement of Philadelphia, December 2015

Deportation, the fate Rosa Robles Loreto sought to avoid, slams the door on an immigrant's life in the United States. It becomes a one-way ticket to the country next door or a flight to a more distant country of origin. Those apprehended by the Border

Patrol may be sent across the border with only their clothes, and if they are lucky, what they were carrying with them.

At the *comedor* in Nogales, Sonora, a dining hall run by the Jesuit priests and Missionary Sisters of the Eucharist of the Kino Border Initiative, recent deportees find a warm welcome, two meals a day, and donated clothing. But the assistance is usually limited to fifteen days. Behind them is another busload of people dropped off with few belongings and many needs.

Most deportees are recent border crossers, said David Hill, a volunteer in Nogales since 2008 with the organization No More Deaths (NMD), located in Tucson. But he meets people in their twenties "who grew up in the United States and speak English better than they speak Spanish" and people in their fifties and sixties "who have lived so long in the US they can't remember anyplace else."

Dorothy Chao, a volunteer with Tucson Samaritans, a desert aid group, and No More Deaths, has met many deportees in Nogales, Sonora, with deep roots in the United States.

"They're devastated," Chao said. "They have no idea what they're going to do."

Because they can't travel to Mexico to visit relatives, undocumented immigrants in the United States might have not maintained family ties, Chao said. This means they may have no one in Mexico to help them after deportation.

Chao coordinates volunteers who drive from Tucson to Nogales, Arizona, and walk across the border to the *comedor* to offer first aid and free phone calls to deportees. In the fall of 2014, shortly after President Obama issued an executive order to shield parents of US citizens from deportation (now on hold in federal court), Chao met a man who had lived in Kingman, Arizona, for more than twenty years. Stopped by a traffic officer, he was eventually deported, leaving his US-citizen wife and two US-born teenagers behind.

"He was trying so hard to be macho and not cry," Chao said. He told her he had a clean record in the United States with no arrests or traffic violations.

Hill also sees people coming directly from the prison system. Many recent border crossers are sentenced to thirty days to six months in prison for illegal entry through a federal court proceeding in Tucson called Operation Streamline. (See chapter 10.) They usually serve their time in private immigration prisons in Arizona and Texas. When the detainees are deported, they get back the money they were carrying in a check or debit card they cannot cash or use in Mexico. Hill and volunteers Juan Manuel and Lupita Aguirre developed a system to cash their checks and cards.[13]

Attorney Margo Cowan has practiced law since 1976, she told the congregation at Southside Presbyterian Church in Tucson in December 2014. In that span, she succeeded in bringing back to the United States only three people who had been wrongly deported.

---

13 "Shakedown," No More Deaths, 2014, http://forms.nomoredeaths.org/abuse-documentation/shakedown/.

In 2010, the Arizona State Legislature passed SB 1070, which required police officers to call immigration officers when they stopped a person they suspected was undocumented. The result was that "more community members were constantly ripped from their homes, work, and communities through deportation," said NMD volunteer Sarah Launius. In response, she, Cowan, and fellow NMD volunteer Kat Sinclair formed Keep Tucson Together (KTT), a legal clinic that offers help to people facing deportation.[14]

In July 2011, John Morton, the former head of Immigration and Customs Enforcement (ICE), provided an avenue. He issued guidelines for how local prosecutors could administratively close cases (prosecutorial discretion), according to Launius.

KTT realized that "people could take steps to stop their own deportations with administrative closure," Launius said. "We have learned how to successfully help individuals fight their own immigration cases and win."[15] Since the legal clinic began in September 2011, its trained volunteers have helped to stop more than one hundred deportations, Launius reported in the summer of 2014.

After President Obama announced the Deferred Action for Childhood Arrivals (DACA) program in the summer of 2012, Launius said that KTT volunteers assisted nearly five hundred youths to apply for DACA. Others did their own paperwork. The legal clinic, held twice a month at Southside Presbyterian Church,

---

14 Denise Holley, "Volunteers Help Stop Deportations to 'Keep Tucson Together,'" No More Deaths, Fall 2014, http://forms.nomoredeaths.org/wp-content/uploads/2014/11/Newsletter-2014-fall-qtz.pdf.
15 Ibid.

is about "empowering people to be able to represent themselves and get their cases closed," Sinclair said.

At the August 2014 clinic, Sinclair noted that there were twenty to thirty "Dreamers" (young people applying for DACA), a couple of bond cases, a couple of asylum cases, and five or six deportation cases. As of 2014 the Tucson immigration court, which includes Douglas, Arizona, was number two in the country in deportation cases closed (Seattle is first), Sinclair said. She cited data from the Transactional Records Access Clearinghouse (TRAC) at Syracuse University.

"Arizona has the highest number of Dreamers," said longtime NMD volunteer Jim Marx. "A lot of credit goes to Keep Tucson Together."

In 2016, KTT closed six deportation cases and helped more than three hundred people complete the naturalization process to become citizens. In early 2017, KTT launched the "People's Power Campaign" to help protect families from raids, detention, and deportation by providing legal counsel and "know your rights" information.

8

Immigrants Organize to Protect Their Community

Rosa Leal stood on a dark street corner on October 8, 2013, in Tucson and watched as protestors joined hands around a Border Patrol vehicle and chanted for the release of the two men inside. Police officers had stopped the men for an unlit license plate and suspected they were in the country without authorization. They called the Border Patrol. Someone alerted people attending meetings nearby at a community center and Southside Presbyterian Church, and those people poured into the street to try to protect the men in custody.

An undocumented resident, Leal stayed back from the action. But she became a target anyway. In the chaos, a Border Patrol agent approached Leal and demanded proof of legal residency. She pulled out her Arizona driver's license, issued before the state required a Social Security number. The agent shook his head and said the license wasn't valid proof. He took her into custody.

At the Border Patrol station, Leal refused to sign a voluntary departure form to be deported and asked to see a judge. She was transported to an immigration detention center in Eloy, Arizona, where she spent two nights. An immigrant advocacy group, *Corazón de Tucson* (Heart of Tucson), raised the $1,500 bond for her release. She and her husband, Eleazar Castellanos, belong to the group of immigrant families that tries to protect its members from arrest and deportation. The organization also bonded out the two men the Border Patrol had apprehended after the traffic stop.

Freedom was costly for Leal. The couple had to come up with $4,500 for a lawyer to fight Leal's case. But after her second hearing in February 2015, her deportation case was closed. A month later, their daughter, Dasia, became a US citizen.

"She gained her permanent residency because she married a citizen," Leal said. Now with her citizenship, Dasia is petitioning for legal status for her mother.

The family came from the Mexican state of Sinaloa but settled in the border town of Nogales, Sonora. In 1996, they entered the United States with border-crossing cards when Dasia was six and moved to Tucson. When the United States changed the crossing cards to a laser document, the family stopped going to Mexico for visits.

"I had a lot of fear," said Castellanos, who now coordinates the day labor center at Southside Presbyterian Church. "I didn't have work, and I had to go out."

SB 1070 put undocumented residents in Arizona on edge. For many immigrants, a trip to the store, workplace, or their children's school became perilous. If they got stopped for a minor traffic violation, then they could find themselves in handcuffs on a one-way trip across the border into Mexico.

Castellanos joined eight other Tucson immigrants, all too familiar with these consequences, in a fast from July 16 through July 20, 2013, to demand an end to this *polimigra* policy. Their action was part of a national *Ni Una Más* (Not One More) fast, sponsored locally by the Tucson Protection Network Coalition.

Southside Presbyterian Church hosted the fasters and their families at the church for the five days. Five participants belonged to the church's day worker center, and several of their coworkers were currently in immigration detention. At a public forum on July 18, the fasters shared several sad stories.

Tucson police stopped Southside worker Manuel Flores Martínez and his wife in November 2012. He spent three months in detention in Florence, Arizona, until supporters raised his bail money. His wife was deported to Nogales, Sonora.

"I don't think any child deserves to see her father arrested," said Ruben Espinosa, who was also stopped. "I felt humiliated."

"What is our crime?" asked Egla Gutiérrez, whose two brothers were deported. "The family is something that God created." When asked if she was experiencing hunger on the third day of the fast, Gutiérrez answered, "I'm hungry for justice."

Castellanos asked President Obama to stop criminalizing immigrants. "I want an end to the indifference," he said.

The fasters invited the mayors and chiefs of police of Tucson and South Tucson to the forum, but they did not show up. The next day, July 19, some sixty-five people delivered a list of demands, drafted by the American Civil Liberties Union (ACLU), to then-Tucson Police Chief Roberto Villaseñor. They asked police to cite and release drivers for minor offenses, not to interrogate passengers, and to allow a friend or relative to pick up the car if the driver is arrested instead of impounding the vehicle.

A change in policy finally emerged, and it came from on high. In November 2014, the Department of Homeland Security (DHS) issued new guidelines that gave priority to deporting convicted felons and suspected terrorists. Villaseñor ordered Tucson police officers to not question crime victims or witnesses about their immigration status or to question a minor without a parent or guardian present. He also told officers to seek alternatives to towing a vehicle, as reported in the *Arizona Daily Star*. These changes fulfilled some of the demands of the fasters, but they required the department to walk a fine line between following federal policy and complying with the state's SB 1070.[16]

In February 2015, the city attorney directed the Tucson Police Department to check for criminal history first before trying to determine immigration status for an individual they stop. No longer

---

16 Perla Trevizo and Luís F. Carrasco, "TPD Revises Immigration Policy," *Arizona Daily Star*, February 25, 2015, http://tucson.com/news/tucson-police-revise-immigration-policy/article_b59466dc-cb05-5c51-94bc-c036478d2eb8.html.

could officers stop an individual solely on suspicion that he or she might be living illegally in the United States.

"They don't bother us as much now," Castellanos said. If one of his workers is stopped, then officers often accept the workers center ID, he said. But he noted that two Southside workers were deported in 2016 for reentry after a previous deportation.

In 2012, *Corazón de Tucson* joined forces with five other community groups from the barrios on the south side of Tucson to form the Protection Network Coalition.

"We are day laborers and domestic workers, mothers and fathers, neighbors, teachers, and whole families," reads a description from the network's website. "We are working to transform our communities and solve the injustices that affect us all."

Castellanos attended a community forum on policing in 2016 and invited new Tucson Police Chief Chris Magnus to meet with the Protection Network. At their meeting, Magnus expressed his desire to work with the immigrant community so they would not fear police officers.

On a practical level, the network strives to "educate people about their legal rights so they can live without fear," said member César González.

"We prepare families in case they face detention," Castellanos said. "What are they going to do with their children so they aren't left alone?"

Protection Network members don't have much money or legal firepower. They fight the steel bars of jail cells with what they can do with their hands: wash cars, sell goods at a yard sale, and prepare food to raise the precious dollars to free a member of their community from detention.

Every August, the network hosts a *pachanga* (party) in Tucson's Armory Park and invites the public to buy food and enjoy music, González said. The money that members raise goes into the network's fund for bonds. Currently, the network, along with allied groups, is pushing the city of Tucson to issue an ID card for residents. This would provide an official card to show if stopped by police, said organizers of Todo Tucson ID. It would benefit undocumented or homeless people, victims of domestic violence, or anyone who moves frequently, and it would help residents use job resources at county libraries.

9

Deport Eleven Million People?

O n the campaign trail, presidential candidate Donald Trump vowed to build a "big, beautiful wall" between and the United States and Mexico and swiftly deport eleven million immigrants living in this country without legal status.

"I don't believe he can do it," said Eleazar Castellanos, coordinator of the Southside Presbyterian Church's workers center in Tucson, about the deportation threat. "I don't think the government of the United States wants to go back to the 1930s when they deported a lot of Mexicans and violated the rights of families with US-citizen children. Afterward, there were problems because US citizens didn't want to do the jobs in agriculture."

Professor Alan Kraut of the history department at American University in Washington, DC, described the plan this way: "Besides despicable, it's impractical…We've put these people to economic use. The money and consumer goods they send home are good for those economies."

Immigration and Customs Enforcement cannot deport all the individuals it estimates to be unlawfully present in the United States with its budget of approximately $6 billion a year. "ICE has prioritized its limited resources on the identification and removal of threats to national security, border security, and public safety," the agency stated in its fiscal year 2015 removal report.

The agency shifted its focus to deport more criminal aliens in fiscal year 2015 (October 1, 2014 through September 30, 2015) as well as those who recently crossed the US-Mexico border. ICE conducted 235,413 removals, the lowest number since 2006. In part, this reflected a much lower number of people apprehended by the Border Patrol: 337,117 in fiscal year 2015.

- In fiscal year 2015, 59 percent of all ICE removals, or 139,368 people, were previously convicted of a crime.
- ICE removed 1,040 individuals who were classified as suspected or confirmed gang members.
- ICE conducted 165,935 removals of individuals apprehended at or near the border or ports of entry.
- Of the 96,045 individuals removed who had no criminal conviction, 94 percent, or 90,106, were apprehended at or near the border or ports of entry.
- Ninety-eight percent of the individuals removed met one or more of ICE's civil immigration enforcement priorities.
- The leading countries of origin for removals were Mexico, Guatemala, Honduras, and El Salvador.[17]

---

17 "ICE Enforcement and Removal Operations Report: Fiscal Year 2015," US Department of Homeland Security, December 22, 2015, https://www.ice.gov/sites/default/files/documents/Report/2016/fy2015removalStats.pdf.

Uprooting and deporting eleven million people who ICE and many US citizens call illegal aliens would be a long and costly process, say the authors of a 2015 study by the American Action Forum, a center-right policy institute. Ben Gitis and Laura Collins estimate the price tag at roughly $400 to $600 billion for deportations and to prevent future unlawful entry into the United States over the next twenty years.[18]

They estimate that 20 percent of these immigrants would pack up their possessions and leave on their own rather than risk a traumatic raid while at home, at work, or in school. That means ICE would forcibly remove at least 8.96 million people.[19]

But those immigrants who do not agree to leave have a right to a court hearing before deportation. (Occasionally, the Border Patrol or ICE detains US citizens or legal residents by mistake if they are not carrying the right documents.) After the undocumented residents are apprehended, they are locked up in a detention center until a judge is available. Currently, the federal immigration courts have a tremendous backlog of cases, many of them for Central Americans seeking asylum, and a shortage of qualified judges to hear the cases.

"As a result, the government would spend $43.5 billion to $243.3 billion to apprehend the undocumented immigrants, $35.7 billion to detain them, $13.4 billion to process them legally, and

---

18 Ben Gitis and Laura Collins, "The Budgetary and Economic Costs of Addressing Unauthorized Immigration: Alternative Strategies," American Action Forum, March 6, 2015, https://www.americanactionforum.org/research/the-budgetary-and-economic-costs-of-addressing-unauthorized-immigration-alt/#ixzz4VNlCx7m1.

19 Ibid.

$11.3 billion to transport them to their home country," wrote Gitis and Collins.[20] The total to deport 8.96 million immigrants would range from $103.9 billion to $303.7 billion.

Transportation costs could balloon because ICE cannot simply bus the deportees to a Mexican border town if they come from a different country. In February 2017, Mexico's foreign minister stated that Mexico would not accept deportees who are not from that country.

"Contrary to popular conception, not all undocumented immigrants are originally from Mexico," wrote the authors. "Pew Research Center reports that in 2012, 52 percent were from Mexico and the rest were from all over the world: 15.2 percent from Central America, 12.4 percent from Asia, 6.3 percent from South America and the remaining were from Europe, the Caribbean, the Middle East, Africa and others."[21]

If the deportations proceed, then the effects would ripple through the US economy for years to come, according to the report. "This would shrink the labor force by…6.4 percent and reduce real GNP [gross national product] by $1.6 trillion in 20 years (5.7 percent)," wrote Gitis and Collins.[22] Deportations would especially disrupt the agriculture, construction, retail, and hospitality sectors.

At least half the undocumented workers in the United States pay federal taxes, wrote the authors, citing estimates from the

---

20 Ibid.
21 Ibid.
22 Ibid.

Social Security Administration and the Congressional Budget Office. "Since this population does not frequently use social services, the loss in tax revenue...would cause the federal deficit to grow."[23]

---

23 Ibid.

10

Are Undocumented Immigrants Criminals?

Three grieving parents and a brother poured out their hearts to a sympathetic audience on opening night of the Republican National Convention in July 2016 in Cleveland, Ohio. Each had lived through the same nightmare: an immigrant in the country illegally had taken the life of his or her beloved family member.

Kent Terry's brother, Border Patrol Agent Brian Terry, was shot in a gun battle with Mexican bandits in southern Arizona in 2010. The assailants fired guns that were later traced to a US government operation called Fast and Furious, run by the Bureau of Alcohol, Tobacco, Firearms and Explosives. ATF had allowed smugglers to take weapons from the U.S. into Mexico to try to hunt down leaders of drug cartels. In the process, the agency lost track of hundreds of firearms.

Mary Ann Mendoza's son, a police officer in Mesa, Arizona, died when an intoxicated man drove the wrong way on a highway and crashed into his car. The immigrant had been convicted of crimes but not deported. In 2012, an undocumented immigrant from Guatemala, deported once for armed robbery convictions and convicted for DUIs, made a turn and crashed his truck into Sabine Durden's son, who was riding his motorcycle, killing him. Jamiel Shaw's son was shot and killed by a gang member who was released from jail, even though federal authorities had asked for a deportation hold on him.

Their grief was real. None of these criminals should have been free to roam the United States or to drive on our highways. But Trump fanned the anger in the auditorium into a sweeping indictment of more than eleven million people who live in the United States without legal status. He painted them as a threat and pledged to enforce US laws. Translation: he would round up and deport millions of hardworking people, even if that action broke up their families and threw their lives into chaos.

Many Americans were incensed in July 2015 when a young woman, Kate Steinle, was shot to death on the San Francisco waterfront. The accused Mexican national who carelessly fired the gun had been deported numerous times. Immigration and Customs Enforcement has made removing "criminal aliens" from the country a top priority. But San Francisco is a "sanctuary city," one of a number of communities that refuse to cooperate with ICE because they don't want immigrants to fear the local police. If local law enforcement joins ICE in raids in immigrant neighborhoods, then when a crime occurs, residents will be afraid to report the incident to police or to give a statement as a witness.

The Department of Homeland Security ended its Secure Communities program in 2014 and replaced it with the Priority

Enforcement Program (PEP) in July 2015. This initiative asks state and local law enforcement to collaborate with ICE to apprehend and deport dangerous individuals who threaten public safety.[24]

Crimes against US citizens by individuals without legal status overshadow the behavior of millions of undocumented residents whose only brush with the law might be a minor traffic violation. Sheriff Tony Estrada of Santa Cruz County, Arizona, has encountered border crossers who became victims of assault and robbery as they tried to migrate to the United States. The veteran lawman said he understands what motivates these impoverished people to leave Mexico and Central America.

"They don't come two thousand miles to be a criminal," Estrada said. "Most people come here with one thing in mind—a better life."

Some 2.7 million undocumented residents found that better life when they legalized their status under the 1986 Immigration Reform and Control Act (IRCA). In 2013, a researcher from Stanford University looked closely at the effects of IRCA on crime in the United States. Scott R. Baker found decreases in crime of 3 to 5 percent, primarily due to a decline in property crimes, equivalent to between 120,000 and 180,000 fewer violent and property crimes committed each year due to legalization. He attributed much of the drop in crime to greater labor market opportunities for applicants.[25]

---

24 "ICE Enforcement and Removal Operations Report," US Department of Homeland Security, December 22, 2015.

25 Scott R. Baker, "Effects of Immigrant Legalization on Crime: The 1986 Immigration and Control Act," Stanford University, April 20, 2013, http://web.stanford.edu/~srbaker/Papers/Baker_IRCACrime.pdf.

Those successful amnesty applicants are now legal residents and citizens of the United States. But those who did not qualify for legalization or who migrated to the United States after 1986 are considered criminals under US laws. What is their crime?

It's called *illegal entry*: crossing the border as a noncitizen without the permission of an immigration official is a misdemeanor that can draw a maximum six-month sentence the first time. Illegal reentry earns a sterner penalty. Returning to or being found in the United States after having been civilly deported or removed is a felony punishable by up to two years in prison.[26]

Some of these penalties are meted out during a federal court process that sentences recent border crossers en masse for illegal entry after deportation. It's called Operation Streamline; it originated in Texas in 2005 and opened in Tucson in 2008. The Border Patrol pushed for this criminalization process as a "deterrence strategy." Lois Martin, a volunteer with No More Deaths, said they wanted to discourage the people they apprehend from reentering the United States illegally. Martin has witnessed these court proceedings, along with others, including members of the Tucson Samaritans, a program of Southside Presbyterian Church.

In Tucson, Operation Streamline hearings in the district federal court process up to seventy-five defendants each day. After a brief meeting with a bilingual attorney, without privacy, almost all the defendants agree to plead *culpable* (guilty) and to serve a prison sentence for the misdemeanor of illegal entry. In exchange, the court agrees to dismiss the felony of reentry after deportation. The

---

26 US Code Title 8, Sections 1325 and 1326.

defendants, chained at the wrists and ankles and smelling of sweat from their desert trek, shuffle in groups to appear before the judge.

Occasionally defendants, especially those from Central America, express fear of being returned to their countries. According to observers from local churches and humanitarian groups, they are really looking for asylum. The judge tells them this is a criminal court and that they can speak with immigration officials about asylum when they finish their prison sentences.

Because many defendants are among the hundreds of thousands deported from all parts of the United States, they may ask to serve their time in a state where family members can visit, Martin said. The judge can make that recommendation, but the Bureau of Prisons decides whether or not to honor the request. Some defendants ask not to serve their sentence in Texas so they will not be deported to a dangerous area of Mexico where they risk extortion and kidnapping.

The defendants serve their thirty-day to six-month sentences in a private prison owned and run by Corrections Corporation of America (CCA, but recently renamed CoreCivic), usually in Florence, Arizona. Any overflow may be sent to a CCA prison in Texas, Martin said. When the detainees finish their sentences, ICE deports them to their countries of origin. Some take the lesson to heart and return to their hometowns. But many will turn around and cross the border again, often desperate to reunite with their families living in the United States or too fearful to remain in their own countries. Only now, the individual bears a criminal record. Will this mean that any future legalization program will exclude these people because of their "crime"?

Crimes such as robbery, assault, rape, murder, and even pos-
session of an illegal drug can put a US citizen behind bars. The
United States has one of the highest incarceration rates in the
world. But immigrants, regardless of legal status, fall way short of
the rate of imprisonment of citizens, according to a report from the
American Immigration Council. Its authors combed through data
from the 2010 American Community Survey (ACS) conducted by
the US Census Bureau. They discovered that "roughly 1.6 percent
of immigrant males age 18–39 are incarcerated, compared to 3.3
percent of the native-born."[27]

The authors stacked the incarceration rate of native-born men
between the ages of eighteen and thirty-nine without a high-school
diploma—10.7 percent—against the 2.8 percent rate among less-
educated Mexican-born men and the 1.7 percent rate among simi-
lar Salvadoran and Guatemalan men. The authors found that the
trend held steady over decades. In census years 1980, 1990, and
2000, the survey revealed incarceration rates for the native-born to
be two to five times higher than rates for immigrants.[28]

The report describes laws that criminalize "an ever-broad-
ening swath of the immigrant population by applying a double
standard when it comes to the consequences for criminal behavior. Immigrants who experience even the slightest brush with the
criminal justice system, such as being convicted of a misdemeanor,
can find themselves subject to detention for an undetermined period, after which they are expelled from the country and barred

---

27 Walter Ewing, Daniel E. Martínez, and Rubén G. Rumbaut, "The
Criminalization of Immigration in the United States," American Immigration
Council, July 13, 2015, https://www.americanimmigrationcouncil.org/
research/criminalization-immigration-united-states.
28 Ibid.

from returning." The authors emphasize that this is would not happen to a citizen.[29]

During his campaign rallies, Donald Trump bellowed that two million criminal aliens were roaming the United States. This poses the question: Who is a criminal alien? A noncitizen who has intentionally harmed or stolen from another person, or a noncitizen simply living in the United States without legal documents who is arrested and perhaps deported after a traffic violation?

---

29 Ibid.

11

Myths about Immigrants

- **The immigrant population in the United States is growing.**

In 2014, people born in another country made up 13.3 percent of the US population of 318.9 million, according to
the Migration Policy Institute (MPI).[30] But there was a time
none of us alive today can remember when the foreign-
born totaled 14.8 percent of the US population. That was
in 1890, and the immigrants were mostly European, according to MPI.[31] Many Americans can trace their ancestry to
those immigrants.

Immigration to the United States took a nosedive in the
1920s, when Congress passed restrictive laws, and continued to drop through the Great Depression and World War

30 Jie Zong and Jeanne Batalova, "Frequently Requested Statistics on
Immigration and Immigrants in the United States," Migration Policy Institute,
April 14, 2016, http://www.migrationpolicy.org/article/frequently-requested-
statistics-immigrants-and-immigration-united-states.
31 Ibid.

II. The number surged after Congress abolished national origin quotas in 1965 and opened the doors to newcomers from Latin America and Asia. The number of immigrants climbed from 9.6 million (5 percent of the population) in 1970 (the historic low as a share of overall population since record-keeping began in 1820) to 42.4 million in 2014. Almost half (47 percent) are US citizens. The rest are lawful permanent residents, people on temporary visas, refugees, asylees, and undocumented immigrants.

- **Almost all undocumented immigrants in the United States come from Mexico.**

There were 5.6 million unauthorized Mexican immigrants living in the United States in 2014, down from 6.4 million in 2009, according to the Pew Research Center.

"Regardless of the exact number of new immigrants from each country arriving in the US each year, the trends are clear: Over the past decade, immigration from China and India to the US has increased steadily, while immigration from Mexico has declined sharply," wrote Ana González-Barrera. "This shift in immigration is noteworthy because since 1965 Mexico has sent more immigrants (16.2 million) to the United States than any other country, in what has been the largest wave of immigration in US history."[32]

---

32 Ana González-Barrera, "More Mexicans Leaving Than Coming to the United States," Pew Research Center, November 19, 2015, http://www.pewhispanic. org/2015/11/19/more-mexicans-leaving-than-coming-to-the-u-s/.

The total number of immigrants living illegally in the United States peaked at 12.2 million in 2007, according to a new study from the Pew Research Center, and then dropped steadily as jobs in the United States dried up during the Great Recession. Mexicans make up a smaller share of that number, about 5.6 million. But that number is nearly offset by an influx of Asians, Africans, and Central Americans.[33]

Since Latinos make up the largest ethnic minority group in the United States, what are the chances any given person of Hispanic descent is undocumented? Not likely, according to MPI.

"The majority of Hispanics in the US are native-born," say the authors of the 2016 MPI report on immigration statistics. "Only 35 percent are immigrants," and many of those enjoy legal status.[34]

- **Legal and illegal immigrants are two separate populations.**

Often they are members of the same family. Sometimes, the father was able to get legal status through employment but brought his wife and children into the country illegally.

---

33 Jeffrey S. Passel and D'Vera Cohn, "Overall Number of U.S. Unauthorized Immigrants Holds Steady Since 2009," Pew Research Center, September 20, 2016, http://www.pewhispanic.org/2016/09/20/overall-number-of-u-s-unauthorized-immigrants-holds-steady-since-2009/.

34 Marc R. Rosenblum and Ariel G. Ruiz Soto, "An Analysis of Unauthorized Immigrants in the United States by Country and Region of Birth," Migration Policy Institute, August 2015, http://www.migrationpolicy.org/research/analysis-unauthorized-immigrants-united-states-country-and-region-birth.

If the couple had more children on this side of the border, then they have US citizens in their family.

When some Americans say they support legal immigration but want to deport those who entered the country without authorization, do they really want to split apart these "mixed-status" families?

- **Undocumented immigrants collect welfare benefits and food stamps.**

This would be virtually impossible. The Personal Responsibility and Work Opportunity Reconciliation Act of 1996 bars almost all federal aid for undocumented residents. Even legally admitted immigrants are ineligible for most assistance for the first five years after arrival. The law makes exceptions for emergency medical care, immunizations, and treatment of communicable diseases.

"In the cash assistance and nutrition assistance [food stamps] programs, benefits are provided only for persons who are either a United States citizen or a noncitizen who meets the federal definition of qualified alien," said James Todd Stone, a public information officer for the Arizona Department of Economic Security (DES).

Stone explained that DES will verify the applicant's immigration status through the US Citizenship and Immigration Services (USCIS) Systematic Alien Verification for Entitlements (SAVE) Program.

The same requirements apply for Medicaid, called AHCCCS in Arizona. A noncitizen without legal status may qualify for federally funded emergency services but not full Medicaid, Stone said. Although it is possible for undocumented families to apply for benefits for their US citizen or legal resident children, most fear drawing attention to themselves and instead focus on working.

A family that wants these benefits must provide proof of citizenship or legal status for those members. "An entire household is not denied just because a noncitizen member is ineligible due to his or her immigration status," Stone said.

- **Undocumented immigrants take jobs US citizens would like to have.**

Harvesting fruit and vegetables with the sun beating down on your back until your hands are scraped and calloused. Grasping chicken guts from an overhead conveyer belt to slap into a pan, over and over again, with the din of machinery filling your ears. Lugging dusty leftovers from a construction site and piling them into a truck. Wiping tables, washing dishes, cleaning motel rooms, or laboring in someone's yard for minimum wage.

These are typical jobs that undocumented workers fill in the United States (although some work their way up to more skilled employment). Most citizen workers are seeking more desirable jobs.

- **All undocumented immigrants want to become US citizens.**

  Many would jump at the chance for citizenship, especially the Dreamers, young people brought to the United States as children who grew up here. But others would be happy just to gain legal residency and permission to work and to have the fear of deportation lifted from their lives.

  Many Americans bristle at offering the undocumented a "path to citizenship" as part of a comprehensive immigration reform, but they might be open to enacting a way for them to earn legal residency.

- **Republicans want to punish people for immigrating without authorization, and Democrats want to help them achieve legal status.**

  While this may be true in most cases, especially in the recent presidential campaign, there are notable exceptions. In 1986, a Republican president, Ronald Reagan, signed the Immigration Reform and Control Act (IRCA), which created a legalization program (often called amnesty) for longtime undocumented residents and farmworkers.

  During a presidential debate with former Vice President Walter Mondale on October 21, 1984, Reagan expressed his support for a pathway to legal status for undocumented immigrants. "I believe in the idea of amnesty for those who have put down roots and who have lived here, even though some time back they may have entered illegally," he said.

But in 1996, Democratic President Bill Clinton signed the Illegal Immigrant Reform and Immigrant Responsibility Act of 1996 (IIRIRA 96). Buried in the multiple changes to immigration law was a provision that barred people from immigrating legally to the United States for ten years if they entered without inspection and stayed for longer than a year. This bar can prevent a US citizen from legalizing the status of an undocumented spouse and may result in deportation (see chapter 6 on the 1996 immigration law).

- **We must secure the border with Mexico before we can grant any legal status to undocumented immigrants in the United States.**

Does this mean seal the border or build a wall so absolutely impenetrable no one can cross except at the ports of entry? Manuel Padilla, chief of the Border Patrol's Rio Grande Valley border sector in Texas, doesn't think this is realistic.

"You're always going to have cross-border crime, period," he told the *Arizona Daily Star* for a special section on border walls. "You're always going to have migration, you're always going to have to deal with the demand for narcotics and the supply of narcotics. We're not in the business of guarantees, but we are in the business of mitigating risk to a level where people feel safe along the border communities."[35]

---

35 Luis F. Carrasco, "Beyond the Wall: Unfenced Borderland Is Mostly in Texas," *Arizona Daily Star,* July 10, 2016, http://tucson.com/special-section/beyond-the-wall/beyond-the-wall-unfenced-borderland-is-mostly-in-texas/article_d1287f84-39a4-11e6-ae8d-973b4788c6c3.html.

Padilla led the patrol's busy Tucson sector from April 2013 to November 2015, according to US Customs and Border Protection.[36]

36 Ibid.

12

Undocumented Immigrants Strengthen the US Labor Force

Current laws in the United States try to defy a basic economic truth: if there is a demand for a product or service, then someone will supply it.

Thousands of Americans crave drugs that are illegal in the United States. Mexican drug cartels feed that appetite by setting up a cross border supply chain to deliver products to their customers. In response, the US government pours billions of dollars into border fences, agents to intercept drug shipments, and eradication of drug crops in their countries of origin. Then our criminal justice system prosecutes nonviolent drug users and sellers and imprisons them. We could take those dollars and try to stem the demand for drugs by offering free treatment for people who are drug dependent.

The demand for immigrant labor is also a strong cross border force, but in a far more positive way. Workers leave areas of Mexico or Central America where they cannot make a living and make a difficult, often hazardous, journey to the United States. They bring farming skills and a strong work ethic to US fields, orchards, packing sheds, and construction sites where their labor is welcome.

This is especially true in the Yakima Valley in Central Washington, where irrigation water flows from the snowpack in the Cascade Mountains onto the fertile soil of orchards and fields of asparagus. But the famous apples and cherries grown here and in the Wenatchee Valley to the north must be tended by capable farm-workers. Since many of them travel from Mexico, the crackdown at the border has taken a large bite out of the agricultural workforce.

"Growers in Washington State reported shortages in 2013 of 8.8 percent in June during the height of the cherry harvest and 8.5 percent in September for apples," reported the *Yakima Herald-Republic*. Ironically, the newspaper noted, 8 percent of Yakima County residents were receiving unemployment benefits and were required to look for work. But somehow, they never connected with the open jobs in agriculture.[37]

Unfortunately, the state's employment security department stopped doing farm labor surveys in April 2014 because of budget cuts, reporter Ross Courtney wrote. The last survey coincided with an early asparagus season and estimated the shortage at nearly 15 percent.[38]

---

37 Ross Courtney, "How Real Is the Farm Labor Shortage?" *Yakima Herald-Republic*, July 11, 2015, http://www.yakimaherald.com/news/local/how-real-is-the-farm-labor-shortage/article_1395de14-2855-11e5-b69f-a3f40e26e59a.html.
38 Ibid.

"If employers are just stealing workers from each other, then that's a pretty good definition of a labor shortage," Mike Gempler, executive director of the Washington Growers League in Yakima, Washington, told the *Herald-Republic*. He estimated a worker shortage of 20 percent during the 2014 cherry harvest, which typically starts in June.[39]

Farm laborers are disappearing from US fields and orchards, according to a report from the Partnership for a New American Economy. A rapid decline in the number of full-time equivalent field and crop workers between 2002 and 2014 cut the workforce by at least 146,000. This represents a drop of more than 20 percent. And it's more difficult for new workers to cross the border into the United States to replenish that labor force: according to the report, their numbers fell by roughly 75 percent between 2002 and 2012.[40]

"The labor shortage has hurt our country's ability to produce labor-intensive fruits, vegetables, and tree nuts," wrote Stephen G. Bronars, the report's author. "Had labor shortages not been an issue, production of these crops could have been higher by about $3.1 billion a year."[41]

Growing crops produces a ripple effect in the whole economy, according to Bronars. That $3.1 billion in additional farm

---

39 Ibid.
40 Stephen G. Bronars, "A Vanishing Breed: How the Decline in Farm Laborers Over the Last Decade Has Hurt the U.S. Economy and Slowed Production on American Farms," Partnership for a New American Economy, July 2015, http://www.renewoureconomy.org/wp-content/uploads/2015/08/PNAE_FarmLabor_August-3-3.pdf.
41 Ibid.

production would have led to almost $2.8 billion in spending on transportation, manufacturing, and irrigation each year, creating more than forty-one thousand additional nonfarm jobs annually.[42]

"There has been a growing demand for low-skilled workers [in sectors such as agriculture, construction, and hospitality]," wrote Michelle Mittelstadt, director of communications and public affairs for the Migration Policy Institute, in an e-mail. "Yet US immigration law sets aside only 5,000 green cards per year for low-skilled workers. So, with demand far exceeding the supply of available legal workers, employers...have turned to unauthorized entries."

Occasionally, the employers get caught. In June 2015, Immigration and Customs Enforcement (ICE) fined Broetje Orchards, an apple grower near Walla Walla, Washington, $2.25 million for its civil violations of the Immigration Reform and Control Act. An audit of the company's hiring records conducted in the summer of 2014 revealed that nearly 950 of the company's employees were suspected of not being authorized to work in the United States.[43]

"We're finding that our big shippers and packers are moving to the H-2A program," said Todd Fryhover, president of the Washington Apple Commission in Wenatchee, Washington. The federal program allows agricultural employers to import workers legally, but they must provide adequate housing.

---

42 Ibid.

43 "Washington Apple Orchard Fined Millions Following ICE Audit," US Immigration and Customs Enforcement, June 4, 2015, https://www.ice.gov/news/releases/washington-apple-orchard-fined-millions-following-ice-audit.

"It's a very costly program," Fryhover said, with transportation expenses and required documentation. Plus, he noted, if the harvest doesn't last long, then the workers cannot be moved to another grower with crops that need picking.

"Over half of the hired workers employed on US crop farms have been unauthorized to work since the mid-1990s," wrote Philip Martin and Linda Calvin.[44]

This puts upward pressure on farm wages, according to Martin and Calvin. If immigration laws are more aggressively enforced, then growers must scramble to find legal workers and to pay higher wages. But if Congress enacts a legalization program, then farmworkers may leave agriculture for better-paying jobs. That would mean growers must pay higher wages to attract workers to their fields.

"In Sonoma County [a wine grape-growing area north of San Francisco], the average farmworker age is going up," said Chris Paige, chief executive officer for the nonprofit California Human Development (CHD) in Santa Rosa, California. "A majority of the workforce remains undocumented and overwhelming Latino." But fewer can be described as migrants, Paige said. In a recent survey, 88 percent of local farmworkers told CHD that Sonoma County was their permanent home.

"There is a lot of fear about what's next," Paige said. "Will these workers have a path to a green card and then citizenship or will

---

44 Philip Martin and Linda Calvin, "Immigration Reform: What Does It Mean for Agriculture and Rural America?" *Applied Economic Perspectives and Policy*, 32, no. 2 (2010): 232–53, https://doi.org/10.1093/aepp/ppq006.

the guest worker model prevail or will the status quo—which is terrible—prevail?"

CHD completed the legalization paperwork for about ten thousand immigrants in Northern California during the 1987–1988 amnesty period, Paige said. The majority were farmworkers, but once they gained legal status, many moved into construction and other better-paying jobs.

Now a shortage of construction workers is squeezing the homebuilding industry, especially in California, Arizona, and Nevada, "where land for subdivisions is plentiful and demand for houses strong," reported Bloomberg News.[45]

Homebuilders try to hire authorized workers but often rely on crews supplied by subcontractors, whose status they can't verify, wrote reporter Prashant Gopal. The Trump presidential campaign insisted there was a "massive pool" of unemployed US workers who could fill the shortage. Approximately 454,000 construction workers were unemployed in August 2016, according to the Bureau of Labor Statistics, the lowest number for August in sixteen years. If builders paid more, then Americans would quickly fill those construction jobs, Gopal wrote, quoting Eric Ruark, director of research at Numbers USA, an organization that favors limiting immigration.[46]

Kevin Moore, who inspects construction sites for Pima County, Arizona, hears superintendents praise their Latino crews who build

---

45 Prashant Gopal, "Trump's Deportation Plan 'Would Be Devastating' for U.S. Builders," *Bloomberg News*, September 14, 2016, https://www.bloomberg.com/news/articles/2016-09-14/mexicans-wanted-why-u-s-builders-hate-trump-s-deportation-plan.
46 Ibid.

homes outside of Tucson. Moore doesn't know the legal status of the workers, but "a lot of them speak very little English," he said.

"They do the jobs Americans don't want to do," Moore said. "And they often do them better and for less pay."

But the workers are not just cleaning up the site or doing general labor, he said. They are performing earthwork, framing the structures, hanging drywall, and roofing homes.

Nationally, undocumented workers hold 34 percent of all jobs in drywall installation, 27 percent in roofing, and 24 percent in painting, said Jeffrey Passel of the Pew Research Center.[47]

Unauthorized immigrants made up 5.1 percent of the nation's labor force in 2012, according to Passel. The 8.1 million workers made up a large share of the total workforce in farming (26 percent), cleaning and maintenance (17 percent), and construction (14 percent). Their share of the workforce peaked at 5.4 percent in 2007, when the Great Recession began.[48]

Undocumented men participate in the US workforce at higher rates than US-born men (91 percent versus 79 percent), Passel said. Only 61 percent of unauthorized immigrant women are in the labor force—many are caring for young children—compared with 72 percent of US-born women. Many US-born adults are not

---

47 Jeffrey S. Passel, "Unauthorized Immigrant Population: National and State Trends, Industries and Occupations," testimony before the U.S. Senate Committee on Homeland Security and Governmental Affairs, Pew Research Center, March 26, 2016, http://www.pewhispanic.org/2015/03/26/testimony-of-jeffrey-s-passel-unauthorized-immigrant-population/
48 Ibid.

in the labor force because they are attending school, retired, or disabled, but that is true for only a small share of unauthorized immigrants.[49]

Since immigration has been stifled in the past twenty years, "the normal economic mobility engine has been disrupted," said Paige of CHD. Usually, an immigrant worker's sons and daughters succeed beyond the level of their parents. But because it is so difficult to cross the border, the undocumented worker must stay in the United States, and family members are often separated for years. "No one has been able to gain legal status," Paige said.

Congress has failed to pass a major reform of immigration policy since 1986. Instead, it relies on the Department of Homeland Security to apprehend and deport migrating workers.

"We'd like to see some action [in Congress]," said Gempler of the Washington Growers League. "We're very much in favor of immigration reform going ahead."

---

49 Ibid.

13

How Immigrants Boost the US Economy

China approaches a crisis as millions of its baby boomers—the largest boomer generation in the world—retire and need support and medical care, reported the PBS NewsHour on August 1, 2016. The country needs a robust generation to provide care and to pay taxes to sustain its elders, said guest Howard French, a former Shanghai bureau chief for the *New York Times*.

But China's one-child policy has dangerously thinned its younger population. Imposed in 1978 to curb population growth, the policy limited couples to one child. It was finally relaxed in 2015. Now, French said, the Chinese realize the policy was a blunder that will limit the resources the country can spend on its military ambitions.

"So, what does that mean the options are for the Chinese government and for the Chinese people?" asked interviewer Judy Woodruff. "How do they reach some sort of equilibrium in terms of having enough people to fill the jobs to keep the engine of their economy going?"

"China, the world's most populous country, 1.3, 1.4 billion people, will in the next decade or so have to begin looking for people outside of China," French replied.

Woodruff observed that China's need for immigrants stands in stark contrast to the situation in the United States.

"The reason the United States is not aging rapidly in terms of its demographics is because we accept people as newcomers to this society in numbers that far surpass any of our major peers or rivals," French said. "And this is what replenishes the workforce. It reinvigorates the society. It underpins our tax base. And so it is this immigration that, in a way, that has been largely unappreciated in our political debate, which really is a kind of churn of our economy."

Immigrants as an asset? Maybe the United States could learn something from this disastrous scenario in China. Our government did not impose any restrictions on family size, but US-born parents usually have fewer children than recent immigrants. Our 74.9 million baby boomers (ages fifty-one to sixty-nine in 2015) are reaching seventy a little ahead of the Chinese generation. Behind them we have Generation X (ages thirty-five to fifty in 2015) approaching 65 million, and 75.4 million millennials (eighteen to thirty-four in 2015). The Census Bureau projects that the Gen-X population will peak at 65.8 million in 2018.[50]

50 Richard Fry, "Millennials Overtake Baby Boomers as America's Largest Generation," Pew Research Center, April 25, 2016, http://www.pewresearch. org/fact-tank/2016/04/25/millennials-overtake-baby-boomers/.

How many workers does it take to support one retiree who is receiving Social Security benefits? When the program was young in 1945 and only a handful of Americans lived to collect their benefits, 41.9 workers supported one retiree. By 1965, Americans were living longer, and the number to support each beneficiary dropped to four workers. By 2010, the ratio dipped to 2.9 workers to each retiree.[51]

Currently, 65.1 million people receive benefits from Social Security programs, according to the booklet "Fast Facts and Figures about Social Security," published by the Social Security Administration. In 2015, an estimated 169 million US workers paid Social Security payroll taxes on their earnings. This represents a ratio of approximately 2.6 workers to each beneficiary.[52]

"The program was stable when there were more than three workers per beneficiary," wrote Veronique de Rugy in a report for the Mercatus Center at George Mason University. "However, future projections indicate that the ratio will continue to fall from two workers to one, at which point the program in its current structure becomes financially unsustainable."[53]

With the Social Security trust fund running low, how can we keep the program solvent? Should we increase the age to receive benefits or raise the payroll tax? It's apparent that America's

51 "Ratio of Social Security Covered Workers to Beneficiaries Calendar Years 1940–2013," Social Security Administration, https://www.ssa.gov/history/ratios.html.

52 Darren Lutz, spokesperson from the National Press Office of the Social Security Administration, in a phone conversation on October 12, 2016.

53 Veronique de Rugy, "How Many Workers Support One Social Security Retiree?" Mercatus Center, May 22, 2012, https://www.mercatus.org/publication/how-many-workers-support-one-social-security-retiree.

working population will have to shoulder a heavier load to fund those who have retired (or become disabled).

If we allow more immigrants now working for cash in the underground economy to step up to better jobs, then they would boost the numbers of employed taxpayers who help to support those sixty-five million beneficiaries and shore up the Social Security system. Currently, this would be illegal. The 1986 immigration law enacted penalties against employers who hire unauthorized workers.

If the United States followed Donald Trump's lead and "subtracted" eleven million undocumented people now living in the United States, then an estimated 8.1 million people would leave our workforce. The figure comes from Jeffrey S. Passel of the Pew Research Center, who estimated the illegal immigrant workforce at 5.1 percent of all workers in 2012.[54]

Fewer unauthorized immigrants live in the United States since the Great Recession began in 2007, and most of them have settled in and become embedded in the economy. A new study by the Pew Research Center gauges the median length of time undocumented immigrants have lived in the United States to be 13.6 years. Certainly, many of these immigrants have children born here and a high stake in staying in this country.[55]

If the United States had opened a pathway to citizenship for its undocumented residents, then the immigrants would have pushed federal revenues $48.3 billion higher from 2008 to 2012. A 2013

---

54 Jeffrey Passel and D'Vera Cohn, "Overall Number of U.S. Unauthorized Immigrants Holds Steady Since 2009."
55 Ibid.

study by the Congressional Budget Office, cited in an economic report in 2013, concluded that most of the gain would have been in Social Security payroll taxes. The immigrants would have cost the United States an estimated $22.7 billion over that period for refundable income tax credits and Medicaid, leaving a federal surplus of $25.6 billion. But the study noted that immigrants would drive up costs for education and health care for state and local governments.

"By bringing immigrant workers out of the shadows, they will be able to obtain above-ground jobs, advance in their careers, and contribute more fully to the economy," said the authors of the report. "Legalizing this population will also benefit US-born citizens as they need no longer compete with workers who may work at below-market wages due to their unauthorized status."[56]

Until April 2016, young immigrants with Deferred Action for Childhood Arrivals (DACA) status in Nebraska were shut out of their career fields in the state where they had lived most of their lives. The state had denied professional and commercial licenses to the students who held work permits because they were not legal permanent residents. State Senator Heath Mello (D-Omaha) described the DACA beneficiaries as "the future of our state" and sponsored a bill to grant them professional licenses, reported the Journal Star in Lincoln, Nebraska. It passed the legislature, but the governor vetoed the bill. After an emotional two-hour debate on April 20, state senators voted 31-13 to override the

56 United States President and Council of Economic Advisers, *Economic Report of the President: Transmitted to the Congress March 2013, Together with the Annual Report of the Council of Economic Advisers* (Washington, DC: US Government Printing Office, 2013), 160.

governor's veto. Dozens of DACA youth seated in the balcony, now free to pursue their careers, rose to their feet and applauded the senators.[57]

---

57 Don Walton and Zach Pluhacek, "Senators override Ricketts' veto on young immigrant licensure bill," Lincoln Journal Star, April 20, 2016, http://journalstar. com/legislature/senators-override-ricketts-veto-on-young-immigrant-licensure-bill/article_a2d6d276-cde0-5d26-a893-dd472c55dc44.html

14

American Dreamers

Imagine you are a child born in a country where your parents do not feel safe or cannot earn enough to feed the family. Your family leaves on a difficult journey to bring you to a country where you have to learn a new language and adapt to a new culture. But wonderful opportunities open up for you if you work hard.

This is what happened to a good friend from college whose family fled Vietnam in a boat in 1980. She had no say over their decision. As refugees from a country the United States fought a war against, the family was admitted legally when my friend was eight. They qualified for resettlement assistance to live in the Seattle area. My friend grew up as a first-generation American, enrolled in college, and earned her degree in pharmacy.

It wasn't easy—she spoke English well, but the written language confounded her. We pored over her assignments, hunting for the right words to answer the questions. It paid off—she graduated and passed her pharmacy exam. She and most of her siblings now work in professional jobs, and her Vietnamese husband owns a popular restaurant. Their experience is a modern-day immigrant success story.

But what happens when a family from the country next door—Mexico—wants to immigrate to the United States? Because our country enjoys a friendly trade and political relationship with Mexico, it's difficult for a Mexican to apply for a refugee visa or claim political asylum. Legal immigration is tightly controlled. If you don't have a close family member or employer to sponsor you, then there is no legal avenue for you to immigrate.

But Mexicans come anyway, just as they did before 1965, when a change in the law made their migration illegal. One such immigrant is nineteen-year-old Martin Valdez of Tucson. He speaks English more readily than Spanish and wants to pursue a career in medicine. In August 2016, he began classes at Pima Community College, the first step in his long journey to become a neurosurgeon.

One circumstance of his life may stand in his path.

"From a very early age, my parents told me we were undocumented and had to be careful," Martin said.

Born into a Yaqui Indian pueblo in Sonora, Mexico, Martin came to Tucson with his parents and younger brothers in 2006, when he was eight. The family found a place to live with relatives on the Pascua Yaqui reservation southwest of town and overstayed their visas. Martin's father had worked for a gas station in Mexico but couldn't earn enough to sustain the family. In Tucson, both his parents found work at a fast-food restaurant, and he and brothers started school—in English.

"I've had amazing teachers," Martin said, and he praised their patience as he worked hard to learn the language and curriculum.

Martin is one of about a million young immigrants brought to the United States as children, schooled here, and immersed in American culture. Since 2001, members of Congress have tried to pass a bill to legalize the status of these youths. It was called the Development, Relief, and Education for Alien Minors (DREAM) Act. But it never came true. In spite of bipartisan support, its sponsors could not muster enough votes in the Senate and House of Representatives to pass the act.

Arne Duncan, Secretary of Education from 2009 to 2015, endorsed the DREAM Act because it would allow "these young people to live up to their fullest potential and contribute to the economic growth of our country" and enable the United States to have the "highest proportion of college graduates in the world by 2020."[58]

In June 2012, President Obama stepped up to protect the youths who would have benefited from the DREAM Act, who came to be known as Dreamers. He issued an executive order to create the Deferred Action for Childhood Arrivals program. For a fee, the program offered work authorization and lifted the threat of deportation for two years and could be renewed. Although many elements of the DREAM Act were reborn in the new program, DACA did not deliver all the act's promises. Without approval from Congress, the order could not pave a pathway for these

---

58 Letter from Arne Duncan to Senator Mitch McConnell, September 21, 2010, https://www.nilc.org/wp-content/uploads/2015/11/ADuncan-ltrs-McConnel-Reid-2010-09-21.pdf

undocumented youths to become legal permanent residents and eventually citizens.

To qualify for DACA, an applicant must have come to the United States before age sixteen; be no older than thirty on June 15, 2012; have lived in the United States for at least five years; be enrolled in school, have graduated, have earned a GED, or have served honorably in the US military or Coast Guard; and be at least age fifteen. An applicant must pass a background check; cannot have been convicted of a felony, a significant misdemeanor, or three or more other misdemeanors; and cannot pose a threat to national security or public safety.[59]

Martin qualified on all counts. His parents were excited and paid an attorney to complete Martin's application. Unfortunately, his official letter never came. Martin said that he lived in legal limbo for two more years until he could renew his status with the US Citizenship and Immigration Services (USCIS). His employment authorization letter finally arrived when he was eighteen and finishing his senior year at Cholla High School. After he graduated in 2015, he went to work at a call center.

"Now that I have the status, I don't feel like I have to hide," Martin said. "I'm allowed to be here. This is the culture I've embraced as my own."

No undocumented immigrants feel so thoroughly American as these Dreamers. By December 2016, the DACA program had lifted

---

59 "Consideration of Deferred Action for Childhood Arrivals (DACA)," US Citizenship and Immigration Services, December 22, 2016, https://www.uscis.gov/humanitarian/consideration-deferred-action-childhood-arrivals-daca#guidelines.

the fear of deportation and given permission to work to 741,546 of these young immigrants.[60]

But the pool of eligible youths is much larger, potentially 1.93 million, researchers at the Migration Policy Institute said in June 2016. Meeting the education requirement stood in the way for 398,000 who could return to school and qualify. Another 228,000 would reach age fifteen in the near future and become eligible for the program.

A large majority of applicants came from Mexico. Natives of Guatemala, El Salvador, Korea, Honduras, China, South America, India, and the Philippines made up most of the other applicants.[61]

With a Social Security card and a DACA work authorization letter in hand, a young immigrant can open a bank account, apply for a credit card, obtain a driver's license, and move up to a better job. Many of them did, said researchers from the American Immigration Council who surveyed 2,684 DACA-eligible young adults between the ages of eighteen and thirty-two in forty-six states and the District of Columbia in 2013.[62]

The DACA recipients who benefited most were enrolled in four-year universities or had graduated with a bachelor's degree,

---

60 Figure quoted by spokesperson from the US Citizenship and Immigration Services on December 9, 2016.

61 "Deferred Action for Childhood Arrivals Data Tools, Data Hub," Migration Policy Institute, 2017, http://www.migrationpolicy.org/programs/data-hub/deferred-action-childhood-arrivals-daca-profiles.

62 Roberto G. Gonzales and Angie M. Bautista-Chávez, "Two Years and Counting: Assessing the Growing Power of DACA," American Immigration Council, June 16, 2014, https://www.americanimmigrationcouncil.org/research/two-years-and-counting-assessing-growing-power-daca.

according to the survey.[63] Colleges in many states offer resident tuition to DACA students, but federal financial aid is off the table. So the students fill that gap the best way they know how: they work.

The researchers discovered that "more than two-thirds of these young adults (67 percent) were employed at the time of the survey, and one-third of our DACA beneficiaries (34 percent) indicated that they held more than one current job. Many of these young people work to contribute financially to their low-income parents."[64]

DACA relieves a young person's fears about being stopped by police, handed over to immigration officers, and perhaps deported, said the researchers. But the protection through DACA does not extend to undocumented family members. They remain at risk of apprehension by the Immigration and Customs Enforcement or the Border Patrol.[65]

While his school and work life are coming together, Martin shares his family's sorrow about the deportation of his mother after a traffic stop in May 2014.

"My dad didn't commit any violations, but the officer pulled over the vehicle because it had Mexican plates," Martin said. At the time, his mother had a valid visa. The family's pastor drove to the scene and tried to dissuade the Border Patrol agent from arresting her.

But the agent took both parents into custody, where they became separated. For a while, family members couldn't find his mother

---

63 Ibid.
64 Ibid.
65 Ibid.

because an agent misspelled her last name, Martin said. When they located her in a detention center in Eloy, Arizona, his aunt drove from Tucson to take the visa to prison officials. He said they kept the document and may have misplaced it. One day, officials called his mother in to sign a stack of papers so she could be released from detention.

"Mom was deported because she signed a voluntary deportation form without realizing what it was," Martin said. She was taken to Nogales, Sonora, when Martin was in his senior year of high school. She traveled south and rejoined members of her extended family in the Yaqui village.

"It's been tough on all of us," Martin said.

With their father still in detention in Florence, Arizona, and no income to pay the bills, the three teenage boys had to move out of their house and stay with relatives.

Ironically, Martin's father was released after a month in custody. The family hired a lawyer, but Martin said the judge ruled that his mother signed the departure form voluntarily. Now their only contact with her is by phone. Martin's father came with him to an immigration clinic on July 7, 2016, to speak with attorney Margo Cowan about his wife's case.

"We actually have a letter from the Mexican government saying we're Yaqui," Martin said, but tribal officials here would not help them. "We have to become citizens first."

He's taken his first steps down that road, but DACA does not offer any path to citizenship, only protection from deportation and permission to work in the United States. It will be up to newly inaugurated President Trump to renew or cancel the executive order that created the program.

The state of Arizona, under former governor Jan Brewer, denied driver's licenses to DACA recipients, arguing they were still not authorized immigrants. District Court Judge David G. Campbell issued a permanent injunction against Brewer's order in January 2015 and gave the green light to thousands of Arizona young adults to drive legally. In April 2016, the Ninth US Circuit Court of Appeals upheld Campbell's decision.

Martin said he looks forward to taking his driver's license exam soon. But his DACA status does not give him the right to receive financial aid for his education.

"Twenty states offer in-state tuition to unauthorized immigrant students, sixteen by state legislative action and four by state university systems," reports the National Conference of State Legislatures.[66]

After a ruling in Maricopa County Superior Court, the Arizona Board of Regents announced that DACA students with a work authorization who live in Arizona may pay the lower in-state tuition. But it's still a hefty sum for a family to afford, and federal financial aid is off-limits for these students.[67]

---

66 Gilberto Mendoza, "Tuition Benefits for Immigrants," National Conference of State Legislatures, July 15, 2015, http://www.ncsl.org/research/immigration/tuition-benefits-for-immigrants.aspx.
67 "ABOR Statement on In-State Tuition for DACA Students," Arizona Board of Regents, May 7, 2015, https://www.azregents.edu/sites/default/files/

Right now, Martin begins his workday at 5:30 a.m. and gets off at 2:00 p.m. He plans to enroll in afternoon or evening classes and continue working forty hours a week to pay for college and to help his family. But how will he and his family pay the tremendous costs of medical school?

That dilemma lies down the road. So does any possible path to citizenship under a new president and changes in Congress. At the immigration clinic, Martin listened to Cowan urge the audience to help turn out the vote to defeat Republican presidential candidate Donald Trump. Martin brightened and said, "That's what I'm looking forward to the most—voting."

Now that Trump has been elected president, those with DACA status live with a new fear: the addresses and personal information they willingly gave to USCIS could be used to trace their location for a future deportation. President Obama created DACA by executive order, and newly inaugurated President Trump could rescind that order. Educators and government officials from around the country are urging Trump to honor the status granted to these promising young people.

---

news-releases/ABOR%20Statement%20on%20In-State%20Tuition%20For%20 DACA%20Students.pdf.

15

Undocumented Immigrants Live Their American Dreams

I think many Republicans are missing the boat when they rail against illegal immigration from south of the border. Most of these immigrants display a strong work ethic, treasure their families, and trust in God to help them in their difficult circumstances. Why wouldn't they be a natural constituency for the Republican Party?

"The illegal alien embodies the American dream," said a grower in an agricultural area where I once lived.

I wonder if some US citizens fear and resent recently arrived immigrants without papers because they are willing to work harder than most of us. They strive to create a better life for their children. Isn't this what our immigrant forebears did for us many generations ago? We live in comfort and relative safety because they labored for us, their descendants. We have forgotten their sacrifices.

Manuel Coppola, publisher of the *Nogales International* and the *Sierra Vista Herald* in southern Arizona, expressed this thought in a post–Independence Day opinion piece:

Daily, thousands leave their homeland to come legally and illegally to the "land of the free and the home of the brave" so they can begin their American Dream—or to get away from violence and oppression. Not much has changed in that regard over the last two centuries.

Throughout most of history there has been backlash against immigrants...I cringe, for example, whenever I hear about a US Customs and Border Protection officer of Mexican heritage mistreating someone at the Nogales port of entry simply because the officer is a citizen but his border-crossing countryman is not. Or what about those second- and third-generation immigrants who vehemently opposed the Dreamers? They got theirs but don't feel that others should have the same privileges.[68]

President Donald Trump is "a man whose version of 'making America great again' includes scapegoating some of the very people who helped make the country so incredible—Latino immigrants," wrote columnist Mary Sanchez of the *Kansas City Star*.[69] Sanchez wrote:

---

68 Manuel C. Coppola, "US Hangover on the Horizon," *Nogales International*, July 5, 2016, http://www.nogalesinternational.com/opinion/editorial/u-s-hangover-on-the-horizon/article_ef04e3e6-3fc4-11e6-bedc-5b49d112c67c.html.

69 Mary Sanchez, "What Latinos Know about America but Donald Trump Doesn't," *Kansas City Star*, May 27, 2016, http://www.kansascity.com/opinion/opn-columns-blogs/mary-sanchez/article80363832.html.

If you want to find someone willing to literally die to become an American, find a recent Latino immigrant. Talk to the Central Americans who risked their lives to come through multiple countries, hoping to gain asylum in the [United States].

They can tell you about yearning for the dignity and freedoms of America, privileges that so many third-, fourth-, or nth-generation Americans take for granted...In a nation that so prides itself on being created from immigrant stock, an awful lot of Americans are naive about migration. Many of Trump's supporters are unaware that their own forefathers did not arrive here with documents in hand, not like what is required now, a system that didn't even exist until recent decades.[70]

In the fall of 2016, I interviewed a Guatemalan immigrant who embraced the American dream by working to ensure that the democratic system works for all Americans, including Latinos. Ben Monterroso gained legal residency through the 1986 amnesty program. In the 1980s and 1990s, he organized workers for the Service Employees International Union (SEIU) in California.

In 1994, Proposition 187 threatened to deny education and health care to California residents without legal status and to report them to immigration officials. SEIU asked Monterroso to lead a campaign against the ballot measure. Monterroso was not yet a citizen and was unable to cast a ballot. But he could motivate others to vote.

California voters passed the proposition, but in 1997, a federal court struck down the law as unconstitutional because it infringed

---

70 Ibid.

on the federal government's exclusive jurisdiction over immigration matters. The law was never implemented. But the electoral victory for Proposition 187 awakened Monterroso and others to the need to mobilize Latino voters.

"Elections matter, the people we elect matter," said Monterroso, now executive director of *Mi Familia Vota* (My Family Votes). "That is why I do what I do."

Monterroso retired from SEIU on a union pension and decided to build *Mi Familia Vota* "so we can be respected and treated like other Americans," he said. His own extended family represents seventeen votes.

After success in California, Monterroso and staff took the *Mi Familia Vota* model to Phoenix, Arizona, in 2004 and later to four other states. He hoped for a national Latino turnout of thirteen to fifteen million for the 2016 presidential election. "We felt like we would be building a tsunami [of Latino voters] by 2020," he said.

Monterroso's proudest moment arrived on September 23, 2015, when he was invited to the White House for the visit of Pope Francis. "The two most powerful men in the world—the first Latino pope and the first African American president—and me," he said. "I can die tomorrow, and I can die happy."

But in November 2016, the expected surge of Latino voters couldn't stave off the electoral-college victory for Trump. As the new president's policies roll out in 2017, the American dreams of so many immigrants could be shattered, and hardworking people could live under a heightened fear of deportation. I fervently hope

Trump will not undo the Deferred Action for Childhood Arrivals program and deport almost 750,000 young people who are working, studying, and serving in the US military. They grew up in this country and make up a vital part of our workforce. They are American in every sense except for their birthplace and immigration status.

If US citizens will rally to support their immigrant neighbors, then we can keep hope alive for those who came here to build their American dreams. We can appeal to Congress to enact reform that opens a way for the eleven million who are left out to gain legal status. We can speak up so that someday these immigrants who belong to America in spirit can finally live here by law.

Epilogue

Rosa Leaves a Lasting Imprint on a Movement to Halt Deportations

Gerardo Grijalva Jr. of Tucson, then eleven, was afraid he would lose his mother in August 2014, before Southside Presbyterian Church opened its doors and took Rosa Robles Loreto into sanctuary. But he didn't know how long she would stay at the church while he, his dad, and his younger brother tried to maintain a semblance of normal life at home without her. He never imagined the turns his young life would take.

"It [Southside] became a second home for us," said Rosa's husband, Gerardo Grijalva Sr.

Pastor Alison Harrington took Gerardo Jr. under her wing and invited him to travel to Washington, DC, with her—twice—to join forces with other immigrants and advocates to press for immigration reform. Gerardo Jr. sat in meetings with members of Congress "to ask them for freedom for people in sanctuary," he said.

In meetings with Representative Raúl Grijalva (D-Arizona) (no relation) and Representative Luis Gutiérrez (D-Illinois), "Gerardo expressed his love for his mother and how devastating it would be to lose her," Harrington said.

During a lobbying visit in December 2014, participants converged on the office of Senator Mitch McConnell (R-Kentucky), the Senate majority leader, and joined hands for a prayer service, Harrington said. Then the senator's chief of staff invited the people into a conference room and listened to their stories of sanctuary.

Rosa stayed in sanctuary longer—fifteen months—than any other immigrant since the recent resurgence of the sanctuary movement, said Nicole Kligerman, a former community organizer for the New Sanctuary Movement of Philadelphia. From 2014 to early 2016, she counted thirteen immigrants who sought sanctuary across the United States.

Offering sanctuary "has been a galvanizing point for people of faith to take seriously the commands of our scripture," Harrington said.

Rosa's experience has inspired undocumented families across the nation, said her attorney, Margo Cowan. "They say, 'We're not leaving...because there's this lady in a church in Tucson, and we're going to follow her witness.'"

Kligerman would agree. "I think the bravery that Rosa and others have shown demonstrates the lengths families will go to and their allies will do to support them," she said.

On November 15, 2015, the Sunday after Rosa walked out of the Southside Presbyterian gates a free woman, she and her family showed up in the sanctuary for the weekly service. With their faces beaming, they worshipped with the congregation that had protected them. Rosa now works for a tortilla factory and cheers for her sons at their baseball games. She and her husband are now safe from the threat of deportation, but she knows other immigrants who live in fear because of Trump's threat to deport a lot of people.

"We have to have patience, have faith, know our rights, and not be afraid," Rosa said. In light of the thousands of immigrants and their citizen neighbors who are uniting to fight deportations, Rosa is hopeful. "Perhaps out of this evil, something good will come."

www.ingramcontent.com/pod-product-compliance
Lightning Source LLC
Chambersburg PA
CBHW070157290526
45789CB00002B/812